Cardiff City Football Club
An A-Z

CARDIFF CITY FOOTBALL CLUB AN A-Z

Dean Hayes

Aureus

First Published 1998

©1998 Dean Hayes

Printed in Great Britain.

A catalogue record for this book is available from the British Library.

Aureus Publishing 24 Mafeking Road Cardiff CF2 5DQ.

ISBN 1 899750 03 7

Foreword

Cardiff City's history is the remarkable one of a club which once had seven internationals in its team, a club that failed to win the League Championship because of a missed penalty in its final match of the season, became the only club outside England to win the FA Cup, and seven years later had to apply for re-election to the Football League.

One can interpret history to show City have been very much a Jekyll and Hyde club - good or bad at times, but never average, and this is particularly true of the last fifteen years when they have won promotion on several occasions from the lower divisions only to fall back again shortly afterwards.

Cardiff City fans, like those of other clubs, enjoy reminiscing about the past, the players who gave them pleasure or filled them with despair, and about who did what, where and when. Cardiff City An A-Z will solve their arguments and will be a source of constant reference for those who follow The Bluebirds.

Richard Shepherd. 1998

Commentator and reporter Richard Shepherd has been following Cardiff City since the mid 1950s and is widely regarded as a leading authority on the Bluebirds.

For Bluebird fans everywhere

Acknowledgments

I should like to express my thanks to the following organisations for their assistance: Cardiff City AFC; The Association of Football Statisticians; The Football League Ltd; The British Newspaper Library; Cardiff Central Reference Library; The Harris Library and Bolton and Blackburn Central Reference Libraries.

Thanks also to the following individuals: Ben Hayes; Iain Price; Harry Williams; Ken Jones; Gareth Davies; Gareth Jones; Robert Lomas; Gareth Williams; Christopher Davies and Dave Twydell. Thanks also to Meuryn Hughes for publishing what is the first book in a series of A-Z books on football clubs.

Dean Hayes

AGGREGATE SCORE

Cardiff City's highest aggregate score in any competition came in the European Cup Winners' Cup of 1969-70 against IF Mjondalen of Norway. The Bluebirds won the first leg in Norway 7-1 to record their best away score in the competition and then triumphed 5-1 at Ninian Park with reserve centre-forward Sandy Allen, who didn't play in the first leg, scoring a hat-trick.

ALLCHURCH, IVOR

Known as the 'Golden Boy of Welsh Football' he began his League career with his home-town club, Swansea Town and made his debut in 1949. Allchurch soon developed a fine understanding with Welsh international inside-forward Billy Lucas and was soon capped himself when he played against England at Roker Park in November 1950.

He became a fixture in the Welsh team for the next 15 years, missing only a handful of games in that time through injury. One of his best games for Wales was against a combined United Kingdom side for the 75th Anniversary of the Football Association of Wales, when he scored twice in a 3-2 win. After he had appeared for Wales in the 1958 World Cup in Sweden, he received great praise from the World's Press and it was obvious that he would soon get the chance to show what he could do in the First Division.

He had scored 124 goals in 330 games for the Swans when Newcastle

United signed him for £27,000 in October 1958. When he arrived at St James' Park, the Magpies were struggling and he had to shoulder much of the club's attacking burden but in four years on Tyneside, he scored 51 goals in 154 games before following the club's relegation, he joined Cardiff City for £18,000.

His first game in City colours saw the Bluebirds draw 4-4 at home to his former club Newcastle United. He scored 12 goals in 35 League games in that campaign, and he was the club's top scorer in 1963-64 and 1964-65.

In 1963-64 he netted his first hat-trick for the club as the Bluebirds held Sunderland to a 3-3 draw at Roker Park. He also scored in the first leg of the Welsh Cup Final win over Bangor City to take City into the following season's European Cup Winners' Cup.

In 1964-65 he scored a hat-trick in a 5-0 demolition of Swansea Town and scored two goals in the second leg of the Welsh Cup Final that saw Cardiff come from behind to beat Wrexham.

At the end of that season, Allchurch, who went on to win his 68th and last Welsh cap in 1966, moved back to Swansea for £6,000 after scoring 43 goals in 126 games for the Ninian Park club. Also in 1966, the Queen presented him with the MBE for his services to Welsh Football.

After ending his League career with Swansea, he played non-League football for Worcester City, Haverfordwest and Pontardawe.

ALLEN, BRYN

After 'guesting' for Cardiff City during the Second World War, Bryn Allen's transfer to the Ninian Park club from Swansea Town was made permanent and he made his League debut in a 2-1 defeat at Norwich City on the opening day of the 1946-47 season.

That season he went on to score 17 goals in 39 League games including a hat-trick in a 6-2 home win over Northampton Town as the Bluebirds won the Third Division (South) championship. He had played in just two games at the start of the following season when he was transferred to Newport County, but a year later he returned to Ninian Park and in 17 League games scored five goals, including four in a five game spell midway through the season.

He left Ninian Park a second time in May 1949 to join Reading but after just nine months at Elm Park, he moved to Coventry City where he scored 26 goals in 88 outings and was capped twice at full international level by Wales.

ALSTON, ADRIAN

The brother of Alec Alston, the Preston North End forward, he emigrated to Australia where he played for the Safeways club. Whilst 'Down Under' he played for the Australian national side which qualified for the World Cup Finals in West Germany in 1974.

His goalscoring exploits for Safeways persuaded Luton Town to give him his chance in the Football League. He had scored eight goals in 29 League outings for the Kenilworth Road club when Cardiff City paid £20,000 for his services in October 1975. He scored two goals on his debut as the Bluebirds beat Chesterfield 4-3 in a seven-goal thriller at Ninian Park. Later that season he became the first post-war Cardiff player to score a hat-trick in the FA Cup when the Bluebirds beat Exeter City 6-2 in a first round tie. In the final game of that 1975-76 season, he scored the only goal of the game as Cardiff beat Bury at Gigg Lane to clinch promotion to the Second Division.

After failing to reproduce that season's form in the Second Division, he left Ninian Park to play in the NASL for Tampa Bay Rowdies, where an injury curtailed his career.

Adrian Alston

ANDERSON, WILLIE

Liverpool-born winger Willie Anderson understudied George Best at Old Trafford after signing professional forms in February 1964. With Manchester United he appeared in two major cup semi-finals - the 1965 European and FA Cup competitions - as Best's replacement. This was quite an achievement because his final tally of first team outings for the Reds amounted to only 12.

He was transferred to Aston Villa in January 1967 for a fee of £20,000 and was ever-present in seasons 1967-68 and 1970-71. His best goalscoring season was 1971-72 when he scored 16 goals in 48 League and Cup games.

He won a League Cup runners-up medal in 1971 and a Third Division championship medal the following season.

In February of 1973 he joined Cardiff City and made his debut in a 3-0 defeat at Swindon Town. Over the next five seasons he became a popular figure with the City supporters, although his best season with the club was undoubtedly the 1975-76 promotion-winning season when his exciting wing play provided a host of chances for Tony Evans and Adrian Alston.

In the summer of 1977, after scoring 12 goals in 126 League games, he left Ninian Park to play NASL football for Brian Tiler's Portland Timbers for a fee of £22,000.

Nowadays, the fast-raiding winger works as an executive with a radio station in Oregon.

ANDREWS, GEORGE

Centre-forward George Andrews was signed from Lower Gornal Athletic in October 1965 and within days of putting pen to paper made his first team debut in a home match against Portsmouth which the Bluebirds lost 2-1. A week later he netted his first League goal for the club in a 2-1 reversal at Bolton Wanderers.

Forming a good partnership with the young George Johnston, Andrews scored 19 League and Cup goals in 36 games in 1965-66 but after scoring six goals in 12 games early the following season, he was allowed to leave Ninian Park and joined Southport.

At Haig Avenue, Andrews scored 41 League goals in 117 games before leaving to join Shrewsbury Town in November 1969.

He continued to score with great regularity at Gay Meadow, finding the net 50 times in 124 League games. He ended his League career with

Walsall where the Dudley-born striker took his tally of League goals for his four clubs to 150 in 437 games.

ANDREWS, JIMMY

Left-winger Jimmy Andrews played Scottish League football for Dundee before joining West Ham United for a fee of £4,750 in November 1951. After five seasons at Upton Park in which he scored 21 goals in 115 games, he joined Leyton Orient before, in the summer of 1959, signing for a Third Division club in Queen's Park Rangers.

At Loftus Road he built a good reputation as a coach and later held that position at Chelsea, Luton Town, Coventry City and Spurs.

It was Frank O'Farrell who brought him to Ninian Park in 1973 but when he left to go to Iran, Andrews took over as caretaker manager. When the Bluebirds avoided relegation, Andrews was appointed on a permanent basis and though they did drop into the Third Division the following year, he brought them straight back again in 1975-76.

After putting the Ninian Park club back on its feet again, they struggled in Division Two, narrowly avoiding relegation in 1976-77.

There was a high turnover of players at Ninian Park and in October 1978 following the unsuccessful coaching appointment of Micky Burns, Jimmy Andrews was sacked.

ANGLO-FRENCH FRIENDSHIP CUP

During the 1961-62 season Cardiff City played Racing Club Lensois over two legs in what was termed the Anglo-French Friendship Cup.

The Bluebirds won both games, 4-2 in France with goals from Peter King (2), Johnny King and Graham Moore, and 2-0 at Ninian Park with Mel Charles and Derek Tapscott the scorers.

APPEARANCES

Phil Dwyer holds the record for the greatest number of appearances in a Cardiff shirt, with a total of 573 games to his credit between 1971 and 1985.

In all, including appearances as a substitute, Dwyer played 471 League games, 23 FA Cup games, 28 Football League Cup games, 45 Welsh Cup games and 6 European matches.

The players with the highest number of appearances for Cardiff City are as follows:

	League	FA Cup	Lg Cup	Welsh Cup	Others	Total
Phil Dwyer	466(5)	23	27(1)	45	6	567(6)
Don Murray	406	23	21	49	33	532
Tom Farquharson	444	36	0	38	0	518
Peter King	352(3)	23	19(1)	45(1)	30(1)	471(6)
Ron Stitfall	402	19	1	32	0	454
*Billy Hardy	353	56	0	34	0	443
*Fred Keenor	369	36	0	31	0	436
Alan Harrington	348	14	11	25	6	404
Alf Sherwood	354	16	0	10	0	380
Len Davies	304	35	0	30	0	369

* Both players made a number of appearances in the Southern League prior to the club's election to the Football League in 1920.

ARRANGED

When Leicester City visited Ninian Park for the final game of the 1948-49 season, seven days after they had lost in the FA Cup Final to Wolverhampton Wanderers, they needed one point to hang on to their Second Division status.

There was nothing at stake for the Bluebirds, but as the game unfolded, it transpired that neither team were prepared to try and win the game.

Billy Baker surprisingly put the Welsh club ahead after 65 minutes but with a little over ten minutes remaining, Leicester equalised after a bad mistake by a Cardiff defender.

The crowd of 35,000 let the teams know how they felt about a game that was certainly not played in the right spirit.

ASHURST, LEN

Liverpool-born Len Ashurst made his name as a constructive full-back for Sunderland, making 410 League appearances for the then Roker Park club before moving to Hartlepool United as player-manager in March 1971. In the summer of 1974 he became manager of Gillingham before joining Sheffield Wednesday in October 1975. Though he made a number of important signings which were of long-term benefit to the Hillsborough side, he left the Yorkshire club in October 1977 with the Owls firmly rooted to the foot of the Third Division without a win in their first ten games of that season.

In the summer of 1978 he was appointed manager of Newport County, helping the Somerton Park club to promotion, the Welsh Cup, and entry into Europe, before moving to Cardiff City. After rebuilding the City side, Ashurst led them to promotion to the Second Division but in March 1984 with the Bluebirds finding life in the higher division harder, he resigned.

He returned to Sunderland as manager but it was an unhappy time for him at his former club and he went abroad to coach in Kuwait and Qatar. He returned to these shores to become assistant-manager at Blackpool before taking full charge at Cardiff City for a second time. The Bluebirds were relegated to the Fourth Division in 1990 and after another poor season, he was dismissed.

ATTENDANCE - AVERAGE
The average home League attendances for Cardiff City over the last ten seasons have been as follows:

1987-88	4,390	1993-94	6,072
1988-89	4,384	1994-95	4,543
1989-90	3,642	1995-96	3,420
1990-91	2,946	1996-97	3,594
1991-92	6,195	1997-98	3,574
1992-93	8,560		

ATTENDANCE - HIGHEST
The record attendance at Ninian Park is 61,556 for the Wales v England international on 14 October 1961 which ended all-square at 1-1. However, the biggest crowd at Ninian Park for a game involving Cardiff City was for Arsenal's visit in a First Division game on 22 April 1953, when 57,893 saw the two sides play out a goalless draw.

ATTENDANCE - LOWEST
The lowest attendance at Ninian Park is 581 when City played against Taffs Well in the Welsh Cup on November 25 1986. The lowest attendance at a league match at Ninian Park is 793 for the visit of Exeter City in an Autowindscreen Shield match on 14 January 1997 which ended 1-1 after extra-time. The Grecians then won 4-2 on penalties.

AUTOGLASS TROPHY
The Autoglass Trophy replaced the Leyland Daf Cup for the 1991-92 season. After a goalless draw against Swansea City at the Vetch Field, two

goals from Carl Dale and another from Chris Pike helped the Bluebirds draw 3-3 at home to Bournemouth and qualify for the knockout stages. In the first round, City travelled to the Victoria Ground where they were beaten 3-0 by a strong Stoke City side.

In 1993-94, City lost 3-0 at Bristol Rovers before goals from Garry Thompson and Phil Stant helped them beat Torquay United 2-0 at Ninian Park. Qualifying for the second round, City travelled to play Wycombe Wanderers where they lost 3-2 after extra-time.

AUTOWINDSCREEN SHIELD

Replacing the Autoglass Trophy for the 1994-95 season, Cardiff City beat Plymouth Argyle 2-0 in their opening match with goals from Griffith and Dale. They then travelled to Exeter City where a Scott Young goal gave them a 1-1 draw. In the second round, the Bluebirds played Exeter City, whom they'd drawn against in their group match. This time the Grecians made the most of the home advantage and beat Cardiff 1-0.

In 1995-96, two goals from Carl Dale and one from Darren Adams who was signed from non-League Danson Furnace, gave City a 3-3 draw at Hereford United. The same combination struck in the next match as Gillingham were beaten 3-2 and though Dale scored from the penalty spot at Northampton in the second round, it wasn't enough to beat the Cobblers, who won 2-1.

The following season, Cardiff won 2-1 at Gillingham. Jeff Eckhardt equalised with the last kick of the game and then after extra-time, a sudden death goal by Carl Dale took the Bluebirds into the second round. Again it took a late goal, this time by Dale to give City a draw in the home match against Exeter City, watched by a crowd of just 793. Unfortunately, Exeter won 4-2 on penalties after extra-time.

In 1997-98, City went out at the first hurdle, beaten 2-0 at home by Millwall.

AWAY MATCHES

Cardiff City's best away win in the Football League came on 29 September 1962 when they won 6-2 at Preston North End. The Bluebirds have scored five goals in a League match away from home on five occasions - Stockport County (5-2 in 1920-21); Burnley (5-1 in 1922-23), Derby County (5-1 in 1965-66), Fulham (5-1 in 1968-69) and Fulham again (5-2 in 1989-90). In the Welsh Cup, Cardiff have scored seven goals in a match on five occasions, winning 7-0 against Pembroke Borough in

1954-55 and Oswestry in 1955-56.

Cardiff's worst defeat away from home is the 11-2 thrashing handed out by Sheffield United on 1 January 1926. Though the Bluebirds also lost 9-0 at Preston North End in 1965-66, the highest scoring away match City have been involved in apart from the Sheffield United game was on 28 April 1962 when they lost 8-3 at Everton.

AWAY SEASONS

The club's highest number of away wins came in season's 1946-47 and 1992-93 when they won 12 of their 21 matches winning the championships of the Third Division (South) and Third Division respectively. The 1992-93 season also saw them score 35 goals away from home to equal the club record established in 1959-60 when they won promotion to the First Division.

The club's fewest away wins came in season's 1932-33 and 1972-73 when they failed to win a game.

B

BADDELEY, LEE

Central defender Lee Baddeley made his debut for his home-town club in the opening game of the 1991-92 season when he came on as a substitute for Gareth Abraham in a 2-1 home defeat by Lincoln City. Capped twice for the Welsh Under-21 side, it was 1993-94 before he established himself as a regular member of City's first team and though he always seemed to

Lee Baddeley

be suffering with head injuries, he still managed to appear in 171 first team games for the Bluebirds. His only goal for the club came in a 3-0 home win over Brighton and Hove Albion on 5 November 1994.

Finding himself third or sometimes fourth choice in the pecking order for a central defensive role, he left Ninian Park in February 1997 and joined Exeter City.

BAKER, BILLY

A former coalminer, Billy Baker had trials with a number of clubs including Arsenal and Wolverhampton Wanderers before joining Cardiff City in 1938. He made his debut at outside-right in a 2-0 home win over Northampton Town in February 1939 but had only made three appearances when the Second World War intervened.

After appearing in 22 wartime fixtures in 1940-41, Baker went to fight for his country but was captured by the Japanese and was a Prisoner of War for almost four years.

When League football resumed in 1946-47, Baker was converted to wing-half and over the next nine seasons, went on to score seven goals in 324 first team appearances. In 1948 he was capped by Wales in the match against Northern Ireland and in 1951-52 was instrumental in helping the Bluebirds win promotion to the First Division. His only goal in that campaign came in the 3-0 home win over rivals Swansea Town.

Baker, who was the only City player to have played before the Second World War and enjoy a lengthy career after it, severed his ties with the club in June 1955 when he signed for Ipswich Town. He spent two seasons at Portman Road, making 20 League appearances before returning to play non-League football for Ton Pentre.

BAKER, COLIN

One of the greatest wing-halves in the history of Cardiff City, Colin Baker replaced his namesake Billy Baker in the Bluebirds side, making his home debut in a 2-2 draw at home to Sheffield Wednesday on the final day of the 1953-54 season. He had to wait until the 1955-56 season before winning a regular place in the City side and over the next ten seasons made 352 first team appearances, including being an ever-present in 1961-62.

The winner of seven full Welsh international caps, he played his first match against Mexico in the 1958 World Cup Finals in Sweden.

Though he was not a prolific scorer, finding the net on just 19 occasions in his Bluebirds career, he did score two goals in the 5-1 home win over

Charlton Athletic on 2 January 1960.

Colin Baker very rarely suffered from injuries but it was he who was the injured player to come off when David Summerhayes became the club's first substitute in the opening match of the 1965-66 season against Bury.

BASSETT, BILL

Centre-half Bill Bassett had played football for Crystal Palace and Wolverhampton Wanderers before arriving at Ninian Park in the summer of 1934. Signed by City manager Ben Watts-Jones, he made his first team debut for the club in the opening game of the 1934-35 season as City beat Charlton Athletic 2-1 at Ninian Park. That season he played in 39 League games and scored what turned out to be his only two goals for the club in a Cardiff career that spanned five years. They came in the 2-1 win over Bournemouth and the 3-3 draw with Bristol City, both at Ninian Park.

The strong-tackling defender was a permanent fixture in the Cardiff side and appeared in 175 first team games up until May 1939 when he rejoined Crystal Palace.

After the Second World War, Bassett continued to play for the Selhurst Park club, making 70 League appearances before returning to Wales to become player-coach of Porthmadog.

BEARE, GEORGE

Right-winger George Beare played his early football with his home-town club Southampton before going to play for Blackpool. His performances for the Seasiders led to First Division Everton signing him in 1911. In three seasons with the Goodison club, Beare missed very few games and when he left to join Cardiff City in 1914, he had scored 19 goals in 118 games.

His first match in Cardiff colours saw City lose 2-1 at Watford on the opening day of the 1914-15 Southern League season. He missed just one game during that campaign as the Bluebirds finished third.

During the war years, Beare played in a number of friendly matches, and on 11 November 1916 scored a hat-trick in a 4-0 win against an International Army XI. He missed just four games in the 1919-20 season, the club's last in the Southern League to take his record in that competition to 15 goals in 75 games.

He made his Football League debut in a 1-1 draw at West Ham United on 2 October 1920 and went on to play in 23 League games that season before leaving to end his career with Bristol City.

BELL, GARY

Gary Bell was spotted playing as an out and out left-winger for West Midlands League side Lower Gornal, but was given his debut at left-half in a match against Wolverhampton Wanderers at Molineux in September 1966. It proved to be a disastrous first match for the Stourbridge-born player, as City lost 7-1, two of which were penalties conceded by himself!

It was Jimmy Scoular who converted Bell into a left-back and it wasn't until 1968-69 that he established himself as a first team regular and formed an outstanding full-back partnership with Dave Carver.

He was ever-present in 1970-71 when the Bluebirds finished third in Division Two and missed just one game in seasons 1969-70 and 1972-73. After losing his place to Freddie Pethard, he went on loan to Hereford United but after just eight games for the Edgar Street club, he signed for Newport County. Bell who had played in 289 first team games was a virtual ever-present in the Somerton Park club's side and made 126 League appearances.

In 1978 he left League football and played non-League football for Bridgend Town and a number of other Welsh League clubs.

BENNETT, DAVE

Winger Dave Bennett started his Football League career with Manchester City. He scored 9 goals in 52 League games and appeared in the 1981 FA Cup Final replay against Tottenham Hotspur before City paid £120,000 to take him to Ninian Park.

After making his debut in a 1-0 win at Barnsley, he played in the same City side as his brother Gary, but despite their presence, the club were relegated to the Third Division. In 1982-83, the Bluebirds won promotion, finishing runners-up to Portsmouth with Dave Bennett scoring 12 goals in 40 League games, including three in the first two matches of the season. He also created many of the chances that Jeff Hemmerman converted to make him the club's top scorer.

After failing to reach agreement over terms, Bennett, who had scored 20 goals in 89 games joined Coventry City, again for £120,000, a figure fixed by an independent tribunal.

At Highfield Road he scored 25 goals in 172 League games and won an FA Cup winners' medal in 1987 as the Sky Blues beat Tottenham Hotspur 3-2. Bennett scored one and made another of the goals as Coventry won their first major honour.

After his departure from Highfield Road, he played for Sheffield

Wednesday, Swindon Town and Shrewsbury Town before leaving the League scene.

BENNETT, GARY

Manchester-born Gary Bennett, brother of Dave, began his career with Ashton United before joining Manchester City in September 1979. Unable to break into the Maine Road club's first team, he joined Cardiff City on a free transfer two years later.

He made his debut in a 3-2 home win over Wrexham two months after arriving at Ninian Park but it was 1982-83 before he established himself as a first team regular. Though he played both in midfield and in attack for the Bluebirds, his best position was in the centre of defence. He had scored 12 goals in 96 first team games when he was transferred to Sunderland for £65,000 in July 1984.

He went on to give the Wearsiders 11 years service and appeared in 463 games, scoring 25 goals. He left Roker Park on a free transfer in November 1995 to play for Carlisle United, but at the end of the season he joined Scarborough. In 1996-97 he played in every match and was voted the North East Player of the Year by the Sunday Sun.

BEST STARTS

The Bluebirds were unbeaten for the first 11 games of the 1923-24 season when they missed winning the League Championship by the narrowest of margins. The club won six and drew five of those 11 matches before losing 3-1 at Preston North End on 27 October 1923.

BIGGEST DEFEATS

The club's biggest defeat in the Football League occurred on 1 January 1926 when they lost 11-2 against Sheffield United at Bramall Lane. They also lost 9-0 at Preston North End on 7 May 1966 and have conceded eight goals on their travels on five occasions - Huddersfield Town (2-8 in 1927-28), Luton Town (1-8 in 1932-33), Luton Town (1-8 in 1936-37), Southend United (1-8 in 1936-37) and Everton (3-8 in 1961-62). The club's worst home defeat was the 9-1 scoreline inflicted on them by Wolverhampton Wanderers on 3 September 1955.

BIGGEST WINS

The club's biggest win in the Football League is 9-2 over Thames Association on 6 February 1932, whilst Enfield were beaten 8-0 in the first round of the FA Cup on 28 November 1931. The Bluebirds have also scored seven goals in a League game on three occasions - Burnley (7-0 in 1928-29), Barnsley (7-0 in 1957-58) and Doncaster Rovers (7-1 in 1997-98).

In the Welsh Cup, Knighton Town were beaten 16-0 on 28 January 1961, beating the club's previous best of 14 March 1923 when Oswestry were defeated 10-0.

BIRD, RONNIE

Erdington-born winger Ronnie Bird began his career with Birmingham City but on finding his first team opportunities at St Andrew's limited, he moved to Bradford Park Avenue where former Newcastle United wing-half Jimmy Scoular was the manager.

His exciting wing-play helped the Yorkshire club consolidate their position in the Third Division following their promotion in 1960-61 but after scoring 39 goals in 129 League games, he left Park Avenue to sign for Bury. His stay at Gigg Lane was only short and in February 1966 he teamed up with Jimmy Scoular again, this time at Ninian Park.

He played his first game for the Bluebirds in a 2-1 defeat at Wolverhampton Wanderers and after establishing himself as a first team regular the following season, won a Welsh Cup winners' medal as Wrexham were beaten 4-3 on aggregate. He won another Welsh Cup winners' medal in 1970 as Chester were beaten 5-0 on aggregate. Bird who possessed a powerful left foot scored in both legs.

He went on to score 36 goals in 130 first team games before being allowed to leave Ninian Park after five seasons with the Bluebirds.

He ended his League career with Crewe Alexandra before joining Gloucester City. He later entered management first with Ebbw Vale and then Bridgend Town.

BISHOP, RAY

Ray Bishop was playing non-League football for Cheltenham Town when City manager Jimmy Andrews paid a nominal fee to bring the Hengoed-born forward to Ninian Park.

He made his League debut in a 3-0 defeat at Blackburn Rovers on 27 August 1977 before going on to play in 22 League games that season. His best season for the club in terms of goals scored was 1979-80 when he shared the leading goalscorers spot with Gary Stevens. At the end of the following season, Bishop who had scored 31 goals in 113 first team games was allowed to join Newport County after Len Ashurst had offered

£10,000 for his services.

Things didn't work out for him at Somerton Park and it wasn't too long before he joined Torquay United. At Plainmoor, he played in 40 games, scoring eight goals before ending his career.

BLACKBURN, GEORGE

Signed by Aston Villa as an amateur from Hampstead Town, one of the best-known amateur clubs in London, George Blackburn turned professional in 1921 and made his League debut at Bradford City in March of that year. A hard-working wing-half, he played in 145 first team games for Villa over a period of six years, picking up an FA Cup Final losers' medal in 1924, the season he played for England against France.

He joined Cardiff City in the summer of 1926 in exchange for Joe Nicholson and made his debut in a 4-3 defeat at Burnley in the opening game of the 1926-27 season. Though he was a regular member of the Bluebirds' side, he missed out on selection for the 1927 FA Cup Final. A firm favourite with the Cardiff fans, he made 132 first team appearances for the club and scored his only goal in a 4-2 home win over Blackpool in February 1930. With Cardiff he won two Welsh Cup winners' medals and a runners-up medal in the same competition.

He left Ninian Park at the end of the 1930-31 season to join Mansfield Town for their first season of League football. He later became player-manager of Cheltenham Town before joining Birmingham City as trainer, a position he held until 1946.

BLACK NOVEMBER

November 1990 was a disastrous month for Cardiff City. Though the Bluebirds beat Chesterfield 2-1 at Ninian Park, they made early exits from the FA Cup where they were beaten by non-League Hayes after a replay and the Welsh Cup where they were well and truly defeated 4-1 at Ninian Park by Merthyr Tydfil. They also lost at home to Exeter City in the Leyland Daf Cup and lost 3-0 at Maidstone and 4-0 at Gillingham in the League.

BLAIR, DOUG

The son of Jimmy Blair, Cardiff City's Scottish international full-back, he began his career with Blackpool but after being unable to break into the Bloomfield Road club's first team, he joined Cardiff City in the summer of 1947.

The inside-forward's first game was at home to Doncaster Rovers on 25

August 1947 which the Bluebirds won 3-0. After that he was a virtual ever-present in the City side for the next seven seasons, scoring 29 goals in 222 first team games. When City won promotion to the First Division in 1951-52, Blair scored eight goals in 28 games and created many more for top scorer Wilf Grant.

When he left Ninian Park he joined non-League Hereford United where he ended his playing career in 1957.

BLAIR, JIMMY

Jimmy Blair began his career in his native Scotland with Bonnybridge Thistle and Glasgow Ashfield before joining Clyde in 1913. Whilst with the Scottish club he was the target for several English clubs, being rated as the best full-back in Scottish football at that time.

In 1914 Sheffield Wednesday paid Clyde £2,000 for his services but they did not get the return they hoped for. This, however, was largely due to unfortunate circumstances. Blair had no sooner arrived at Hillsborough when he was injured in a motorcycle accident and suffered another accident soon after that. He had only played in 20 first team games for the Owls when football was suspended because of the First World War and he returned to Scotland. The Hillsborough club had quite a job persuading him to move south again after the war, for Blair wanted a better deal than the Yorkshire club could offer. When he finally returned, he found himself in a side doomed to relegation. In April 1920 he was in the Scotland side beaten 5-4 by England in an epic rain-swept international at Hillsborough but seven months later he joined Cardiff City for £3,500.

After making his debut for the Bluebirds in a 4-2 win at Blackpool, he went on to give the Welsh club six years service, appearing in 175 League games. He was in the City side which lost to Sheffield United in the 1925 FA Cup Final and earned six full international caps for Scotland during his stay at Ninian Park.

In 1926 he joined Bournemouth and made 61 appearances for the Cherries before retiring two years later. He returned to Ninian Park in a coaching capacity in 1932 before returning to the licensing trade.

BLAKE, NATHAN

The powerful striker began his career with Newport County before being taken on as a trainee by Chelsea. Unable to break into the first team at Stamford Bridge, he returned to South Wales and began his League career with his home-town club Cardiff City.

17

He made his debut for the Bluebirds in a 2-1 defeat at Bristol Rovers in March 1989 before establishing himself as a first team regular the following season. Over the next three seasons, Blake was a virtual ever-present and in 1992-93 when the club won the Third Division championship, he scored 11 goals in 44 League games. He had scored 14 goals in the first 20 League games of the 1993-94 season including a hat-trick against Stockport County to take his tally to 40 goals in 164 games when Sheffield United paid £300,000 to take him to Bramall Lane.

In his first full season with the Blades, he top scored with 17 goals in 35 League games and led the way again in 1994-95 with 12 goals in 22 League outings before Bolton Wanderers paid £1.35 million for his services in December 1995.

Blake won his first full international cap against Norway in 1994 before scoring on his full debut in Moldova, but in his first season at Burnden Park he only found the net once, in a 4-1 win at Middlesbrough, the club's first away victory in the Premier League.

Nathan Blake

He came into his own in 1996-97, forming a prolific goalscoring partnership with John McGinlay, scoring 24 League and Cup goals as the Wanderers returned to the top flight. Despite the Lancashire club being relegated for a second time in three years, Blake was the club's top scorer. His strength on the ball and turn of pace continued to make him a firm favourite of the fans.

BONSON, JOE

A big and burly centre-forward, Joe Bonson began his career with Wolverhampton Wanderers and though he did appear in 10 League games during his four years at Molineux, he played the majority of his football in the club's Central League side.

The Bluebirds had just transferred Johnny Nicholls to Exeter City and signed Bonson as his replacement for a fee of £7,000. He made a goalscoring debut in a 1-1 home draw against Ipswich Town in November 1957. That season he scored 12 goals in 25 League games. He formed two formidable striking partnerships, first with Ron Hewitt and then from 1958-59 with Derek Tapscott, following his arrival from Arsenal.

Bonson's best season in terms of goals scored was 1959-60 when he netted 18 goals in just 26 matches including scoring two goals in three consecutive games - Lincoln City (Home 6-2), Hull City (Home 3-2) and Leyton Orient (Away 4-3). At the end of that campaign, Bonson who had scored 43 goals in 85 games for the Ninian Park club was exchanged for Scunthorpe United's Peter Donnelly.

Bonson who scored the majority of his goals with his head, netted 11 goals in 52 games for Scunthorpe before playing for a number of clubs - Doncaster Rovers, Newport County, Brentford and Lincoln City. His best spell was at Somerton Park when he scored 47 goals in 99 games for the Ironsides.

The Barnsley-born centre-forward played in 328 League games for his six clubs and scored 131 goals.

BOYLE, TERRY

A Welsh Schoolboy international, he began his career at Tottenham Hotspur but failed to make the grade with the White Hart Lane club and moved across London to play for Crystal Palace. At Selhurst Park he made 26 League appearances and had a short spell on loan at Wimbledon as well as being capped twice at full international level by Wales before being transferred to Bristol City. He had played in 37 League games for the Ashton Gate club when he was given a free transfer and joined Newport County to ease the club's financial difficulties.

One of the best defenders ever to play for the Somerton Park club, he scored 11 goals in 166 League games before joining Cardiff City for £22,000 a fee fixed by an independent tribunal.

He made his debut in a 1-1 draw at Hartlepool United on the opening day of the 1986-87 season and was ever-present during that campaign in which City finished 13th in the Fourth Division. Boyle was ever-present again in 1987-88 as the Bluebirds won promotion to the Third Division and won a Welsh Cup winners' medal when City beat Wrexham in the final. He went on to appear in 101 consecutive League games from his debut and in 167 first team matches altogether before leaving to end his League career with Swansea City.

BRITTAN, CHARLIE

Charlie Brittan was probably the best right-back in the Southern League when Tottenham Hotspur signed him from Northampton Town in October 1911. Having begun his career as a 16-year-old with Portsmouth he moved to Northampton and in five years with the Cobblers made five appearances for the Southern League in inter-league matches.

However, at White Hart Lane he was never sure of a first team place and after playing in 53 games he demanded a transfer. His request was granted and in November 1913 he moved back to the Southern League with Cardiff City. He made his debut in a 2-1 win at Swindon Town on 20 December 1913 and held his place in the side for the rest of that season. He was a virtual ever-present in the club's Southern League team either side of the First World War, playing in 88 games.

As Captain of the Bluebirds' side that played in the club's first Football League match at Stockport County, he played in 36 games in the 1920-21 season and led the side into the First Division. He made two appearances for the Welsh League and helped City win the Welsh Cup in 1920 and 1922. He had played in 75 League games when he lost his place to Jimmy Nelson. After a career in business, he later went into politics as a member of Cardiff City Council.

BROTHERS

There have been a number of instances of brothers playing for Cardiff City. Albert Keating began his League career with Newcastle United but made his name with Bristol City before having a short spell with Blackburn Rovers. He scored 23 goals in 47 games for the Bluebirds before returning to the north-east to play non-League football. His younger brother Reg Keating also started with Newcastle before spells with Stockport County, Birmingham City and Norwich City. He joined Cardiff some 18 months after his brother had left Ninian Park. He scored 36 goals in 70 games including four in a 5-0 home win over Exeter City on 27 April 1935.

Ron Stitfall is one of Cardiff's greatest-ever players. A Welsh international, winning two caps, he was a regular partner to Alf Sherwood at fullback and made 403 appearances for the Ninian Park club. Though his brother Bob was on Cardiff's books, it was the smallest of the three, Albert who played in the club's first team. Though he only made nine appearances, he did score the only goal of the home game against Grimsby Town in 1949-50.

Without doubt the greatest Welsh footballer of his generation, John Charles had already made his name with Leeds United, Juventus and Roma before arriving at Ninian Park in 1963. His younger brother Mel followed him to Elland Road but soon returned to South Wales to play for Swansea Town. He later joined Arsenal before signing for the Bluebirds in 1962. They played together on a number of occasions and in the friendly against Juventus in May 1964 both got on the scoresheet in a 3-3 draw.

One of the club's most loyal servants, Richie Morgan, who for most of his playing career understudied Don Murray and later became manager ,appeared in 69 League games for City, several of which were with his younger brother Peter, who failed to make much of an impression and left to continue his career with Hereford United.

Welsh international David Giles had two spells with the Bluebirds and made 109 League appearances. In between his spells, his younger brother Paul made his debut but failed to make the most of his rather limited chances.

Gary Bennett joined the Bluebirds on a free transfer from Manchester City and proved to be one of the club's most versatile players before leaving Ninian Park to join Sunderland. His brother, Dave Bennett, also joined the club from Manchester City for £120,000. The two were important members of the Cardiff side that won promotion to the Second Division in 1982-83 and both scored in successive home wins over Walsall and Millwall.

BROWN, BOBBY

Whilst playing for Barnet, centre-forward Bobby Brown won England amateur international honours before joining Fulham. His stay at Craven Cottage was short and he joined Watford where he scored 10 goals in 28 League games before moving to Northampton Town. He continued to score for the Cobblers, netting 22 in 51 League outings before Cardiff City paid £15,000 for his services in October 1966.

He made his debut in a 4-2 home defeat by Hull City. He then went on to top score with 15 goals in 29 League games to help the Bluebirds avoid relegation to the Third Division, despite being at the foot of the table for much of the season. In that campaign, he won a Welsh Cup winners' medal, scoring in the first leg as Wrexham were beaten 4-3 on aggregate. He continued to find the net in 1967-68 and had scored nine goals in 21 League games when he injured a knee in the 3-0 home win over Aston Villa on Boxing Day. In fact, Brown who scored 31 goals in 64 games for the Bluebirds was never to play League football again, so badly damaged was his knee.

BUCHANAN, JOHN
Scottish midfielder John Buchanan played his early football for Ross County in the Highland League before coming south of the border to play for Northampton Town. He soon won a place in the Cobblers' first team and in four years at the County Ground, scored 25 goals in 114 League appearances.

John Buchanan

In October 1974, Buchanan moved to Ninian Park in exchange for John Farrington and made his debut in a 3-2 home win over York City. At the end of that season, the Bluebirds were relegated but bounced back in 1975-76 when a late unbeaten run resulted in the club winning promotion to the Second Division. Though Buchanan played all his games in midfield, he topped the club's scoring charts on two occasions with a best of 16 in 1978-79 when the Welsh club finished ninth in the Second Division. That season saw him score his only hat-trick for the club in a 4-0 home win over Sheffield United.

Buchanan finally left Ninian Park in 1981 after scoring 67 goals in 265 games to return to the County Ground to see out his career with Northampton Town.

BURROWS, FRANK

A tough, uncompromising defender, Frank Burrows began his football career with Raith Rovers before entering the Football League with Scunthorpe United in the summer of 1965. He went on to make over 100 League appearances for the Irons before joining Swindon Town for a fee of £12,000 in 1968. He helped the Robins win promotion to Division Two as

Frank Burrows

runners-up and to a shock League Cup victory over Arsenal in 1969. His playing career ended in October 1976 when after 298 League appearances for the Wiltshire club, he became Swindon's assistant-manager.

He later went into coaching, but after joining Portsmouth in 1978 he succeeded Jimmy Dickinson as Pompey's manager and in his first season in charge, the club won promotion to the Third Division. He stayed until 1982 when he became coach at Southampton, later taking up a similar post with Sunderland.

He took over at Ninian Park in May 1986 as the Bluebirds entered the Fourth Division for the first time. City were runners-up in 1987-88 but he left to work as assistant to John Gregory at Portsmouth. When Gregory left, Burrows took control of the club for a second time before becoming manager of Swansea in 1991. The Swans reached the Second Division play-offs in 1992-93 but in 1995 he lost his job.

He returned to Ninian Park for a second spell as City manager in 1998.

C

CAMPBELL, ALAN

The Arbroath-born midfielder began his career with Charlton Athletic and in five seasons at The Valley made over 200 League and Cup appearances before joining Birmingham City in October 1970 for a fee of £80,000.

The Scottish Youth international won Under-23 honours whilst at St Andrews and soon settled into one of the club's finest sides.

Campbell hardly missed a game for Birmingham, playing in 175 League games and scoring 11 goals before Cardiff manager Jimmy Andrews paid £20,000 for his services.

Adept at finding space and fine at passing the ball, Alan Campbell was also a distinctive figure on the field of play with his long dark hair and a shirt which always looked far too big for him !

After making his debut in a 1-1 draw at Chesterfield, he played in the last 14 games of the 1975-76 season and was only on the losing side once when City were promoted to the Second Division.

One of the most popular players at the club, he appeared in 190 first team games in almost five years at Ninian Park before leaving in November 1980 to join Carlisle United where injury forced him to leave League football.

CAPACITY

The total capacity of Ninian Park in 1997-98 was 14,980.

CAPTAINS

The club's first captain was Davy McDougall who joined the Bluebirds from Glasgow Rangers as player-manager. He had played football in Scotland and Ireland and had experience with Bristol City. He helped the club recruit a number of players that he knew the club would need to survive in the Southern League. He left Ninian Park at the start of the 1912-13 season to become player-manager of Newport County.

Charlie Brittan was Cardiff's captain when they entered the Football League in 1920-21. The former Tottenham Hotspur player went on to play 75 League games for the Welsh club before he lost his place to Jimmy Nelson.

The greatest captain in the history of Cardiff City is Fred Keenor who led the club to victory in the 1927 FA Cup Final and to second place in the First Division. The Cardiff-born half-back played in 369 League games for the club before joining Crewe Alexandra in 1931.

After Fred Stansfield had captained the club to the Third Division (South) championship in 1946-47, Alf Sherwood led the side with great determination for a number of years and in 1951-52 helped the club win promotion to the First Division. He played in 353 League games before joining Newport County where he appeared in a further 205 League games.

Danny Malloy captained City when they won promotion to the First Division again in 1959-60. He was an inspirational leader and he even scored two own goals in the club's 3-2 win over Liverpool on the opening day of the season. Also among the many players who have captained the club is Phil Dwyer, who holds the club appearance record with 573 first team games.

CARVER, DAVID

David Carver began his League career with his home-town club Rotherham United, and after establishing himself in the Millmoor club's first team, went on to make 83 League appearances before leaving to join Cardiff City in January 1966 for a fee of £11,000.

Strong in the tackle and a good distributor of the ball, he played his first match in Cardiff colours in a 1-1 draw at Bury and over the next six seasons was a virtual ever-present, playing in 269 first team games for the club. He won Welsh Cup winners' medals in four successive seasons from 1968 to 1971 and was ever-present in season's 1969-70 and 1970-71 when he appeared in 93 consecutive League games.

Carver's only goal for the Ninian Park club came on 17 October 1970 when he hit one of the goals in a 2-2 draw against Leicester City in a match featured on BBC Television's 'Match of the Day' programme.

After leaving the Bluebirds he had a short loan spell with Swansea before joining Hereford United on a free transfer. He later returned to Yorkshire to end his League career with Doncaster Rovers.

CASSIDY, PAT

Giant centre-half Pat Cassidy joined Cardiff City from Bradford City in the summer of 1912 and made his first team debut at Swansea Town on the opening day of the 1912-13 Southern League season. It was Swansea's first Southern League match and ended all-square at 1-1. That season, Cassidy missed just one game, a goalless draw in the home fixture against Swansea when the Bluebirds won the Championship and promotion to the First Division of the Southern League. Two of Cassidy's four goals that season came in the record-breaking 9-0 victory over Ton Pentre.

Cassidy was a virtual ever-present in the club's Southern League days up until the outbreak of the First World War but when the game resumed in 1919-20 he only appeared in five games, being replaced by Bert Smith, an Irishman from Donegal. Cassidy appeared in 89 Southern League games for the Ninian Park club and scored 11 goals.

CENTURIES

There is just one instance of an individual player having scored 100 or more League goals for Cardiff City. Len Davies is the greatest goalscorer with 128 strikes in his Bluebirds career (1919-1931).

Don Murray holds the record for the most consecutive League appearances - 146. Other players to have made over 100 consecutive League appearances during their careers are Arthur 'Buller' Lever (114), Barrie Jones (107), Alf Sherwood (101) and Terry Boyle (101).

CHAMPIONSHIPS

Cardiff City have won a divisional League Championship on two occasions. The first was in 1946-47 when Stan Richards set a new club record with 30 goals as the club won the Third Division (South) championship without losing a single game at Ninian Park. The club lost just six games including the first of the season at Norwich and established the record of eight successive away wins. Also during that 1946-47 season, the club scored 93 goals, their highest total in the League.

The Bluebirds last won a divisional championship in 1992-93 when they finished three points ahead of runners-up Wrexham in the Third Division, losing just once at home.

CHARITY SHIELD

On 12 October 1927, Cardiff City played the famous amateur side Corinthians at Stamford Bridge in the FA Charity Shield. The Corinthians side was a strong one, containing many representative players and it was no surprise when they took the lead just after half-time through Ashton. Hughie Ferguson equalised for the Bluebirds in the 78th minute and with just five minutes remaining, Cardiff's professional fitness told as Len Davies scored the winning goal.

CHARLES, JOHN

Immense in physique and talent, John Charles proved to be the complete footballer with a calm and unruffled temperament which earned him the nickname of 'The Gentle Giant'.

Charles was plucked from his native Swansea by Leeds United manager Major Buckley in January 1949 and within three months had made his League debut for the Elland Road club. Despite having to undergo two cartilage operations before he had reached 21, his impact and influence on the game were both immediate and lasting.

At the age of 18 years 71 days, he became the youngest international to play for Wales when he took to the field against Northern Ireland in March 1950, the first of 38 caps.

As the Yorkshire club bid for more goal power in an effort to climb out of the Second Division, Charles was moved from centre-half to centre-forward and in 1953-54 he scored 42 goals in 39 League games to become the first Welshman to top the Football League scoring lists.

Eventually hard-up United had to sell John Charles who had scored 157 goals in 327 games to Juventus who paid a world record fee of £65,000 to take him to Turin at the end of the 1956-57 season.

In Italy he became an idol overnight, scoring 30 League goals to pick up a Championship medal and the Italian Footballer of the Year award in his first season. He won two more Championship medals plus three Italian Cup medals and Italian League representative appearances. After 108 goals for Juventus he returned to Elland Road in August 1961 in a £53,000 deal but did not settle and when AS Roma bid £70,000 for him, he returned to Italy.

In August 1963 he joined Cardiff City and made the most remarkable debut for the Bluebirds. Charles scored from fully 75 yards as Norwich City were beaten 3-1 at Ninian Park and he went on over the next two and a half seasons to score 19 goals in 88 games.

In 1965 he became Hereford United's player-manager, helping to lay the foundations of the club's successful bid for Football League status.

After spells on the Swansea coaching staff, he ended his involvement with football as manager of Merthyr Tydfil.

CHARLES, MEL

The younger brother of the legendary John Charles, Mel Charles signed professional forms for Swansea Town in May 1952 and over the next seven seasons played in over 250 first team games as well as winning 21 Welsh caps, including playing in the World Cup Finals of 1958.

In March 1959, Arsenal paid a club record fee of £40,000 to take him to Highbury. He spent his first season with the Gunners alternating between centre-half and centre-forward before two cartilage operations hampered his progress. He had scored 28 goals in 64 League and Cup games when he was transferred to Cardiff City for £20,000.

He made his debut in a goalless home draw against Manchester City in March 1962 and over the next three years went on to appear in 103 first team games. When asked to play in attack he always scored goals, although he did equally as good a job in defence.

Surprisingly, he was allowed to leave Ninian Park by manager Jimmy Scoular in the summer of 1965 and after a spell with Porthmadog, he returned to League action with Port Vale.

CHISHOLM, KEN

Ken Chisholm was a fighter pilot during the Second World War. He joined Queen's Park in 1945 and the following year turned out for Scotland in a Victory international against Northern Ireland. He left Hampden Park in 1946 for Partick Thistle and the legendary Major Frank Buckley, manager of Leeds United signed him from Partick in January 1948.

He stayed at Elland Road for less than a year before moving to Leicester City with whom he won his only honour, an FA Cup runners-up medal in 1949.

In March 1950 he signed for Coventry City and soon became a great favourite at Highfield Road. In 1950-51, his only complete season with the Sky Blues, he netted 24 goals, most of them before Christmas. He had scored ten the following term but by March 1952, Coventry were strug-gling to avoid relegation and in a desperate attempt to revive his ailing side, Harry Storer sold him to Cardiff City.

He made his debut for the Bluebirds in a disastrous 6-1 defeat at Sheffield United but then proceeded to score eight goals in the last 11 games of the season to help the club end the campaign as runners-up and gain promotion to the First Division. For the next two seasons, he was the Ninian Park club's leading scorer and on 31 October 1953, scored his only hat-trick for the club in a 5-0 home victory over Charlton Athletic.

He left Cardiff in 1954 after scoring 33 goals in 63 League games to play for Sunderland and later Workington. In January 1958 he became Glentoran's player-manager.

Chisholm was one of the players involved in the Sunderland illegal payments scandal of the 1950s. He was suspended *sine die* for refusing to answer the investigating committee's questions. Subsequently he admitted receiving illegal payments and forfeited his benefit qualification terms.

CLARK, BRIAN

Brian Clark began his League career with his home-town club Bristol City and in six years with the Ashton Gate club, scored 83 goals in 195 League appearances. At the end of the 1965-66 season, he was allowed to leave and joined Huddersfield Town. Unable to settle at the Yorkshire club, he was snapped up by City manager Jimmy Scoular for the bargain fee of £8,000.

He scored twice on his debut when the Bluebirds won 4-3 at Derby County and then netted again the following week on his home debut when Preston North End were beaten 2-0. Forming a formidable partnership with John Toshack, he netted 17 League goals in 1968-69 and won the first of three successive Welsh Cup winners' medals before being one of three ever-presents in 1969-70. That season Clark topped the club's League scoring charts and in the Welsh Cup tie against Barmouth and Dyffryn scored five goals in City's 6-1 win. In 1970-71, Clark again headed the club's scoring list with 15 League goals but it was his goal that defeated Real Madrid 1-0 in the European Cup Winners' Cup quarter-final first leg that ensured his place in the history of the club.

The following season he was the club's leading scorer for a third successive term with a total of 21 League goals. In 1972, he and Ian Gibson were somewhat surprisingly allowed to leave Ninian Park and joined Bournemouth for a combined fee of £100,000. After twelve months at Dean Court, he joined Millwall before returning to play for the Bluebirds.

In that 1975-76 season, he helped the club win promotion to the Second Division and win his fourth Welsh Cup winners' medal but after scoring 108 goals in his two spells with the club, he left to end his League career with Newport County.

Brian Clark heads Cardiff's 12 minute winner
Cardiff City 1 Real Madrid 0 - March 1971 - European Cup Winners' Cup Quarter Final 1st leg (Att: 47,500)

CLARKE, ROY

Roy Clarke's first taste of international recognition was as a member of the Welsh Schools Baseball team in 1939. During the Second World War he worked in the coal-mines but managed to play football for a local side at weekends. He later joined Cardiff City and became a prolific scorer during the wartime games, netting 69 goals in 129 outings. In 1946-47 he was an important member of City's Third Division (South) championship winning team, scoring 11 goals in 39 games before leaving to join Manchester City.

He holds the unique record of playing in three different divisions of the Football League in three consecutive League games! He played his last game for the Bluebirds in their penultimate game of the 1946-47 Third Division (South) season and then played in Manchester City's last game of their Second Division promotion winning season against his home-town club Newport County. Clarke's next game with the Maine Road club came in the top flight at the start of the 1947-48 season when Wolves were beaten 4-3.

He won his first international cap for Wales against England in 1948 and his last eight years later against Northern Ireland. He made 22 appearances for his country, scoring five goals. With Manchester City he won an FA Cup winners' medal in 1956 but after scoring 73 goals in 349 League games, he moved to Stockport County where he ended his League career.

CLEAN SHEETS

This is the colloquial expression to describe a goalkeeper's performance when he does not concede a goal. Danny Canning in 1946-47 had 23 clean sheets from 40 League appearances when the Bluebirds won the Third Division (South) championship.

CLENNELL, JOE

A little demon on the ball, Joe Clennell played in junior football in his native north-east with the likes of Silksworth United and Seaham Harbour before entering the Football League with Blackpool. Then he played for Blackburn Rovers before joining Everton in January 1914.

Making his debut at home to Aston Villa at the end of the month, he scored Everton's goal in a 4-1 defeat. On the opening day of the 1914-15 season he scored a hat-trick as the Blues beat Tottenham Hotspur 3-1 at White Hart Lane. He went on to score 17 goals in 41 League and Cup appearances when the club won the First Division championship and reached the semi-finals of the FA Cup.

In wartime football, Clennell scored 128 goals in 124 games for Everton, including four in a match on five occasions ! When the Football League resumed in 1919, he continued to find the net with great regularity and scored a hat-trick in a 4-1 home win over Bradford City.

In October 1921, Clennell signed for Cardiff City and made his debut in a 2-2 draw at West Bromwich Albion. Over the next four years, Clennell scored on a regular basis with his best season being 1922-23 when he found the net 14 times in the League including a hat-trick in a 5-1 win at Burnley. After losing his place to Harold Beadles he joined Stoke before moving to Bristol Rovers and Rochdale. He was only staying briefly anywhere at this time, but his affinity with Wales showed through when he became player-manager of Ebbw Vale, then Barry Town and Bangor before going to Great Harwood. He later managed Distillery in the Irish League and coached Accrington Stanley.

COLLINS, JIMMY

Somewhat on the small side for a centre-forward, Jimmy Collins began his career with Tooting and Mitcham before being given his chance in the Football League with Queen's Park Rangers. He failed to make much of an impact at Loftus Road and returned to non-League football with Tunbridge Wells. He proved to be a prolific scorer with the Kent club and so was given another chance at League level by Rochdale. He later had spells with

Stockport County and Liverpool before signing for Cardiff City in 1937.

He scored City's goal in a 1-1 draw at Clapton Orient on the opening day of the 1937-38 season and then netted a hat-trick on his first appearance at Ninian Park as Torquay United were beaten 5-2. He ended the season as the club's top scorer with 23 goals in 39 League games as City finished 10th in the Third Division (South). He headed the scoring charts again in 1938-39 with 18 goals in 36 League appearances including his second hat-trick for the club in a 5-3 home win over Watford.

He scored four goals in the three League matches that were played in the abandoned season of 1939-40 and then scored seven goals in 12 wartime games to take his Cardiff record to 59 goals in 108 games before the hostilities ended his Ninian Park career.

COLOURS

The first known colours of Riverside were chocolate and amber quartered shirts and black knickers but by the time the club, now known as Cardiff City played their first match in a friendly against Aston Villa to open Ninian Park on 1 September 1910, the team were wearing blue shirts, white shorts and blue stockings.

The club's present colours are blue shirts, white sleeves, white shorts and white stockings, whilst the change colours are yellow shirts, black shorts and yellow stockings.

CONSECUTIVE HOME GAMES

Cardiff City played an extraordinary intense sequence of six home games in succession in just 25 days (1 November - 25 November 1988) and won them all without conceding a goal !

Date	Opponents	Competition	Score
01.11.1988	Bury	Division Three	3-0
05.11.1988	Gillingham	Division Three	1-0
12.11.1988	Northampton Town	Division Three	1-0
15.11.1988	Bath City	Welsh Cup	3-0
19.11.1988	Hereford United	FA Cup	3-0
25.11.1988	Brentford	Division Three	1-0

CONSECUTIVE SCORING - LONGEST SEQUENCE

George Johnston holds the club record for consecutive scoring when he was on target in six consecutive League games. His first came from the penalty spot in a 3-2 defeat at Norwich City on 28 August 1965 and ended with two goals, including the winner in a 4-3 victory over Manchester City at Ninian Park on 18 September.

CRICKETERS

The only Cardiff City players who were cricketers of real note were Joe Hills, Ernie Carless, Stan Montgomery and Ron Nicholls.

Joe Hills who kept goal for City in 14 League games in the mid 1920s, played as a professional batsman for Glamorgan from 1926 to 1931, scoring 3,252 runs at an average of 20.58. He hit six centuries, the highest being 166 against Hampshire at Southampton in 1929. From 1939 to 1956 he was on the first-class umpire's list and in 1947 stood in the fourth Test at Headingley between England and South Africa.

Ernie Carless played in two League games for Cardiff City but appeared in the majority of the club's wartime games and turned out in the game against Moscow Dynamo in 1945. He appeared in just three games for Glamorgan scoring 35 runs at 11.66 before playing minor county cricket for Devon. He returned to Ninian Park in later life as the club's groundsman.

Stan Montgomery who appeared in 231 League games for the Bluebirds between 1949 and 1950, played cricket for Essex Second XI before joining Glamorgan. He scored 763 runs at 18.60 for the Welsh county and took six wickets at a cost of 16.50 runs apiece.

Ron Nicholls kept goal for both Bristol clubs and in 59 first team games for Cardiff City. He played first-class cricket for Gloucestershire and scored 23,606 runs at 26.17 with a highest score of 217 against Oxford University in 1962, a season in which he scored 2,059 runs. In 1966, his benefit year, he hit a hundred before lunch in the Gillette Cup match against Berkshire.

CURTIS, ALAN

Alan Curtis began his Football League career with Swansea Town and took part in the Vetch Field club's steady climb from the Fourth Division to the First, winning 14 Welsh caps on the way. He had scored 72 goals in 248 League games for the Swans when he was transferred to Leeds United for £400,000, a record for a player from the lower divisions. Sadly for him and Leeds, injury and a loss of form restricted his career at Elland Road to just 28 League appearances and he rejoined Swansea.

In November 1983, Southampton manager Lawrie McMenemy spent £80,000 to take the Welsh international to The Dell and though he continued to win caps for his country he never really produced his early Swansea form for the Saints. Failing to hold down a regular first team spot, he had a loan spell at Stoke City before returning to Wales to play for Cardiff City.

He played his first game for the Bluebirds in a goalless home draw against Rochdale in the second game of the 1986-87 season and went on to play in 40 League games. The following season he was instrumental in the club winning promotion to the Third Division and the Welsh Cup, in which he scored one of the goals in a 2-0 win over Wrexham. He continued to be a regular member of the first team in 1988-89 but during the early part of the following season after which he had scored 13 goals in 157 games, he returned to the Vetch Field for a third spell, after which his career drew to a close.

Alan Curtis

CURTIS, ERNIE

A former Cardiff and Welsh schoolboy footballer, he worked as an electrician whilst continuing to play amateur football. During the 1925-26 season,

Cardiff gave him the opportunity to show what he could do as an amateur triallist. After winning an Amateur cap, he was offered full-time terms and made his League debut in a 2-0 home defeat by Manchester United in September 1926. He held his place for most of the season as the Bluebirds advanced to the FA Cup Final against Arsenal. He played out of position on the right-wing as first choice Willie Davies had been taken ill earlier on that season. He was, at that time, the youngest player ever to appear in a Cup Final, aged only 19 years. He added a Welsh Cup winners' medal a few weeks later when City beat Rhyl 2-0 to round off a fairytale first campaign.

In October 1927 he won his first full Welsh cap against Scotland at Wrexham and scored in a 2-2 draw.

In 1928, Fred Stewart sold him to Birmingham for £3,000, thus beginning a five year stay which was to see him make a second Wembley appearance in 1931 in the all-Midland final against West Bromwich Albion which Birmingham dominated but lost 2-1.

In November 1933 he returned to Ninian Park but his stay was short-lived after he became involved in a dispute with manager Watts-Jones over the amount of wages he had been promised. He then joined Coventry where he also had a spell as player-coach before returning home at the outbreak of the Second World War in 1939.

He joined the Royal Artillery but was captured by the Japanese and made a Prisoner of War from 1941 to the end of the hostilities. On his return to Britain, he joined City for a third spell, this time as the club's Reserve Trainer, a post he held until he left the game in the early 1960s.

D

DALE, CARL

Carl Dale began his career with Bangor City before joining Chester City for a fee of £12,000 in May 1988. In three seasons with the then Sealand Road club, he scored 48 goals in 139 first team games, prompting the Bluebirds to pay £100,000 to bring him to Ninian Park.

He made his debut at Crewe Alexandra on 24 August 1991, scoring City's goal in a 1-1 draw. Forming a deadly partnership with Chris Pike, he top scored for the club with 22 goals but City could only finish ninth in the Fourth Division. After helping the club win promotion in 1992-93 when he scored 11 goals in 35 outings, he struggled with injury for a couple of seasons before being back to his best in 1995-96.

During that campaign, he scored 30 goals, 21 in the League, including a hat-trick in a 3-2 home win over Doncaster Rovers and nine in the various cup competitions. Despite not being fully fit in 1996-97 his four goals in the final five games of the season took the club into the play-offs. Again, he suffered with injuries in the 1997-98 season, but Dale, a forward who is always dangerous, even when not completely fit, took his total of goals for the club to 103 in 263 first team games.

DAVIES, FRED

Liverpool-born goalkeeper Fred Davies began his career with Llandudno Town before signing for Wolverhampton Wanderers in 1957. Initially, he was unable to break into the first team at Molineux and he spent four seasons in the club's Central League side before being given his chance. He went on to play in 156 games for Wolves before being transferred to Cardiff City in January 1968 for a fee of £10,000.

He kept a clean sheet on his debut as Portsmouth were beaten 3-0 at Ninian Park and ended the season with a Welsh Cup winners' medal as Hereford United were beaten in the final. In 1968-69 he was an ever-present as the club finished fifth in the Second Division and won his second Welsh Cup winners' medal as Swansea City were beaten 5-1 on aggregate. He missed just two League games in 1969-70 but at the end of the season after which he had played in 128 first team games, he joined Bournemouth.

He went on to play in 134 League games for the Dean Court club before coaching at a number of clubs.

DAVIES, LEN

The only Cardiff City player to have scored over a century of League goals for the club, Len Davies joined the Bluebirds in 1919 before they were elected to the Football League. He played in just one Southern League fixture in that 1919-20 season when City drew 2-2 at Luton Town. He made his Football League debut in the club's inaugural season in the competition in a 2-0 win at Barnsley, but it was 1921-22, the club's first season in Division One, following their promotion, that he came to the fore. Replacing Fred Pagnam, he scored 17 goals in 25 League games including a hat-trick in a 6-2 home win over Bradford City. That season he won a Welsh Cup winners' medal after scoring four goals in a 7-1 defeat of Newport, a hat-trick in a 5-0 win over Merthyr Town and one of the goals in the final as Ton Pentre were beaten 2-0.

In 1922 he won the first of 23 caps for Wales when he played against England.

In 1922-23 he headed the club's League goalscoring charts with 19 goals in 27 games including scoring a hat-trick in a 6-1 defeat of Chelsea. Also that season he won another Welsh Cup winners' medal and netted another hat-trick in a 10-0 win over Oswestry. In 1923-24 he again topped the scoring list with 23 League goals including all four in a 4-2 win at West Bromwich Albion. At the end of that season, he missed a late penalty at Birmingham. Had he converted, it would have given City the League Championship. Topping the scoring charts for the third consecutive season in 1924-25, he netted another hat-trick in a 4-1 home win over Bury.

Following the arrival of Hughie Ferguson, Davies found himself playing out wide and though the goals dried up, he was still in sparkling form. In 1926-27 he helped the club win both the FA Cup and Welsh Cup, scoring one of the goals in the 2-0 win over Rhyl in the final of the latter competition.

He continued to be a virtual ever-present for the club until 1930-31 when after scoring 184 goals in 369 games, he left Ninian Park to play for Thames Association. The following season, he was in the Thames side City defeated 9-2 to record their best League win but after netting 12 goals in 27 games he returned to Wales to become player-manager of Bangor City.

DAVIES, WILLIE

After playing his early football with Rhymney, he joined Swansea Town in 1921 and played in all the forward positions before settling at outside-right. Davies who won 17 Welsh caps, collected his first against Scotland in February 1924 when he scored in a 2-0 win at Ninian Park.

With the Vetch Field club in severe financial difficulties, Davies joined Cardiff City in the summer of 1924 for just £2,500. He made his League debut for the Bluebirds in a 2-1 defeat at Birmingham City in September 1924 and missed just a handful of games before playing in the 1925 FA Cup Final against Sheffield United. Though not a prolific scorer, netting 19 in 98 League and Cup games for City, the most important of these came in the last minute of the fourth round tie that season when the Bluebirds faced Leicester City at Ninian Park. His in-swinging corner-kick flew directly into the Leicester net for the winning goal of a tense 2-1 encounter ! A serious chest illness caused him to miss the 1927 FA Cup Final but he later recovered and was transferred to Notts County.

After making 71 appearances in two years at Meadow Lane, he joined Tottenham Hotspur, missing only four of the next 105 League and Cup games. However, with age beginning to creep up on him, he only played in 15 games when Spurs won promotion in 1932-33 and at the end of the season he returned to Swansea where he played for three years before finishing his career at Llanelli.

DEBUTS

Neil O'Halloran is the only player in the club's history to score a hat-trick on his League debut when he netted all the goals in a 3-1 win over Charlton Athletic on 10 December 1955.

Gary Bell conceded two penalties on his debut for the Bluebirds on 21 September 1966 in a 7-1 defeat against Wolverhampton Wanderers at Molineux.

Phil Bater has the unenviable distinction of being the only Cardiff City player to be sent off on his debut when he received his marching orders in the 3-0 defeat at Wrexham on 12 September 1987.

DEFEATS - FEWEST
During the 1946-47 season, the Bluebirds went through the 42 match programme and only suffered six defeats as they won the Third Division (South) championship.

DEFEATS - MOST
Cardiff's total of 27 defeats during the 1933-34 season is the worst in the club's history. Not surprisingly, they finished bottom of the Third Division (South).

DEFEATS - WORST
Cardiff's record defeat was when Sheffield United beat them 11-2 at Bramall Lane on New Year's Day 1926. The Bluebirds have also had nine goals put past them on two occasions. On 3 September 1955, Wolverhampton Wanderers beat City 9-1 at Ninian Park to equal the record Division One away score and on 7 May 1966, City travelled to Deepdale and were beaten 9-0 by Preston North End, the club's record post-war defeat.

On 17 November 1945, City entertained Moscow Dynamos, who were on a short tour of Great Britain. Though it was a makeshift Bluebirds' side, the Russian side inflicted on the club their worst ever home defeat by winning 10-1.

DEFENSIVE RECORDS
Cardiff's best defensive record was established in 1946-47 and helped the club win the Third Division (South) championship. They conceded just 30 goals in that campaign and were beaten in only six matches.

City's worst defensive record was in 1933-34 when they let in 105 goals to finish bottom of the Third Division (South).

DIBBLE, ANDY
Andy Dibble played his first game for the Bluebirds on 5 May 1982, his 17th birthday, in a 1-0 home defeat by Crystal Palace. The following season, manager Len Ashurst gave him an extended run in the side as the club challenged for promotion. City were unbeaten in 17 of Dibble's 20 appearances in that 1982-83 campaign and when they ran out at The Valley for their

opening game in the Second Division against Charlton Athletic, Dibble was the club's first-choice 'keeper. He missed just one game in that 1983-84 season, his impressive performances alerting a number of clubs. Luton Town were at the head of the queue and in the summer of 1984 he joined the Kenilworth Road club for £125,000, a fee fixed by a tribunal.

However, competition for a place was tight and he had various loan spells. He will always be revered by Hatters fans for his crucial penalty save against Arsenal at Wembley when Luton won the 1988 Littlewoods Cup.

The Welsh international 'keeper joined Manchester City for £240,000 in July 1988 but a serious groin injury in March 1989 disrupted a fine season. A pre-season broken leg in 1992-93 was a further setback and though Tony Coton's consistency limited his chances, he made 115 League appearances for the Maine Road club before joining Rangers in March 1997. He played in the last seven games of the campaign, helping the Ibrox club win the Scottish League title.

DISMISSALS

In the opening match of the 1925-26 season at Maine Road, Scottish international Jimmy Nelson became the first Cardiff City player to be sent off in a Football League match following a last-minute flare-up with Manchester City winger Johnson. The referee awarded the home side a penalty from which they scored the winning goal to triumph 3-2. To make matters worse, Nelson received a four-week ban and missed seven matches.

During the Welsh Cup competition of 1959-60, the Bluebirds drew Swansea Town in the sixth round. Because they had an important League fixture at Leyton Orient two days later, they tried to get the date of the tie changed but the Welsh FA refused the request. Bill Jones decided to field a Reserve side whilst Swansea fielded their Second Division team. With Cardiff surprisingly leading 2-1 in this Vetch Field encounter, Colin Hudson was sent off for committing a foul and then with just five minutes remaining, the Bluebirds were reduced to nine men when Steve Mokone and Swansea's Harry Griffiths were given their marching orders after throwing mud at each other !

In the sixth round of the 1973-74 Welsh Cup, Irish Amateur international Bill Irwin became the first Cardiff City goalkeeper to be sent off. The Bluebirds were leading 3-0 at Oswestry when in the last minute, the home side were awarded a penalty. The normally placid 'keeper protested so strongly that he was dismissed.

On 28 February 1979, Lindon Jones at 17 years 361 days became the youngest player to be sent off in Cardiff's colours in their 4-1 win at Blackburn Rovers. The only Cardiff City player to be sent off on his debut is Phil Bater who was dismissed on 12 September 1987 in a 3-0 defeat at Wrexham.

DIVISION THREE (SOUTH) CUP

The club first entered this competition in 1933-34 but lost at home to Aldershot in the first round 1-0. It was the same story the following season, the Bluebirds losing 3-1 at Crystal Palace with Tommy Vaughan netting City's goal. In 1935-36, the club were again paired with playing Crystal Palace at Selhurst Park and though John Diamond gave them an early lead, they lost 2-1. The Bluebirds went out at the first hurdle for the fourth season in succession in 1936-37 when they went down 1-0 at home to Exeter City. The following season, City eventually won a game in the competition when Bert Turner scored the only goal at Northampton Town. In the second round for the first time, City travelled to Ashton Gate but lost 2-1 to Bristol City. The Bluebirds travelled to Ashton Gate again in 1938-39 for what not only transpired to be their heaviest defeat, 6-0, but also their last-ever game in the competition.

DRAWS

Cardiff City played their greatest number of drawn League matches in a single season in 1997-98 when 23 of their matches ended all square. 16 of their matches ended all-square in seasons 1950-51, 1973-74 and 1986-87. Their fewest draws were in seasons 1946-47 and 1983-84 when only six of their matches were drawn.

The club's highest scoring draw is 4-4, a scoreline in six games - Derby County (Home 1927-28), Millwall (home 1930-31), Bournemouth (Away 1935-36), Stoke City (Home 1959-60), Newcastle United (Home 1962-63) and Plymouth Argyle (Away 1985-86).

DURBAN, ALAN

A skilful midfield player, Alan Durban began his Football League career with Cardiff City and made his first team debut in September 1959 in a 2-1 win at Derby County, the club with which he was to make his name. He had scored nine goals in 52 League outings when Tim Ward the Derby County manager paid £10,000 for him in July 1963.

Durban had two distinct phases at the Baseball Ground, the first as a goalscoring inside-forward and the second as an intelligent midfield player.

In 1964-65, both he and Eddie Thomas scored 24 goals and Durban went on to score 112 goals in 403 games for County, including four hat-tricks. However, his best days for Derby were in midfield. His greatest attribute was an ability to find space in a crowded penalty area, arriving late to score a large percentage of his goals from close range.

He had earned 27 Welsh caps by the time he left Derby to join Shrewsbury Town, where he became player-manager. After steering them out of the Fourth Division in 1974-75 and later into the Second Division, he left Gay Meadow to manage Stoke City. He took the Potters into the First Division and then had a couple of troubled seasons with Sunderland before being sacked in March 1984.

In September 1984 he moved back to his first club, Cardiff City as manager but it turned out to be a bad move. His spell at Ninian Park saw the club plummet from the Second to the Fourth Division and in May 1986 he left the club to run an indoor tennis club in Telford.

DWYER, PHIL

One of the Cardiff City greats, Phil Dwyer holds the club record for the number of appearances with a total of 573.

A member of the successful Bluebirds' youth team of 1971, the former Welsh Schoolboy international made his debut for the City first team in a goalless draw at Orient in October 1972. He held his place for the rest of the season and ended the campaign with his first Welsh Cup winners' medal when Bangor City were beaten over two legs. An ever-present in 1973-74, he won another Welsh Cup winners' medal and played in 76 consecutive League games from his debut until injury forced him to miss a game.

In 1975-76 he missed just one game - a 4-1 defeat at Hereford - as the Bluebirds won promotion to the Second Division. At the end of that season he won his third Welsh Cup winners' medal, scoring two goals in the first leg against Hereford United, in a tie City won 6-5 on aggregate.

Never one to shirk a challenge, he won Under-21 and Under-23 honours before winning the first of 10 full caps for Wales against Iran in 1978.

Despite a series of niggling injuries, he missed very few games and in 1983-84, he was an ever-present. Though the majority of his 573 games were played at full-back or in the centre of defence, he still managed to score 50 goals. City manager Alan Durban let him leave Ninian Park towards the end of the 1984-85 season and he joined Rochdale where he played in just 15 League games.

Phil Dwyer

E

EARLY GROUNDS

Originating from the Riverside Cricket Club, Cardiff City formed a team in 1899 and played their early matches at the cricketer's ground within Sophia Gardens. After three years, the footballers moved to a stony pitch at Roath before disbanding but then re-emerged in 1905 back at Sophia Gardens. A year later, the club tried to adopt the name Cardiff City but were informed by the local FA that the title should be kept for the first Cardiff team to turn professional. Before taking such a step, the club decided to gauge public opinion by staging a series of friendly matches. The first two were played at Cardiff Arms Park against Crystal Palace of the Southern League and Bristol City, then in the First Division of the Football League. The third against Middlesbrough was at the Harlequins Ground, Newport Road. Delighted with the level of public interest, the club decided to turn professional and find a permanent home.

EDWARDS, GEORGE

One of football's outstanding wingers of the 1940s, George Edwards began his career as an amateur with Swansea and made his first team debut towards the end of the 1938-39 season. Before the outbreak of the Second World War he won a Welsh Amateur cap against England. During the war years he continued to play for Swansea whilst studying for a Degree at Swansea University but when he was called up for the RAF he was stationed in the Midlands and 'guested' for Coventry City.

In 1945-46 he played for Wales in the Victory Internationals and in October 1946 he won his first full cap against Scotland.

By now Edwards was a Birmingham City player and though he only scored nine goals in 84 League games for the St Andrew's club, they were usually very important goals.

In December 1948 he joined Cardiff City for a fee of £12,000 and made his debut in a 2-2 draw at Leicester City. An ideal replacement for Roy Clarke who had left Cardiff for Manchester City in 1947, he was a member of the team that won promotion to the First Division in 1951-52, providing a number of chances for both Chisholm and Grant. He went on to score 34 goals in 194 League games but netted hat-tricks in the 7-1 Welsh Cup win at Bangor in March 1951 and in a 6-1 win against the Jersey Saturday League in a friendly two months later.

When he made the decision to leave the game in 1955, he was still City's first choice and playing well. He was later invited to join the Ninian Park club's Board of Directors, a position he held for nearly 30 years.

ENGLAND, MIKE

Beginning his Football League career with Blackburn Rovers, Mike England was soon acknowledged as arguably the best young centre-half in the country. He made his debut for Wales against Northern Ireland in April 1962 and by the time he had played the last of his 165 League games for the Ewood Park club and joined Spurs for a fee of £95,000 in August 1966, he had won 20 full caps to go with 11 at Under-23 level.

The fee was a British record for a defender and England who was to be Spurs' defensive kingpin for the next nine seasons, hardly missed a game except through injury. In his first season he helped the White Hart Lane club lift the FA Cup and later played his part in the 1972 UEFA Cup and 1973 League Cup successes. He captained his country and won a further 24 caps whilst with Spurs but with the club struggling against relegation, he quite suddenly announced his retirement.

However, he re-emerged the following August to play for one season with Cardiff City, having spent the summer with Seattle Sounders. After missing the opening game of the season, a 2-0 defeat at Grimsby Town, he made his debut in a 1-1 home draw against Bury before going on to make 40 League appearances and help the club win promotion from the Third Division.

Strong, quick and brave, England left Ninian Park at the end of that season when a proposed coaching job at the club fell through.

He spent four further American summers playing for Seattle and appearing for Team America in the 1976 Bi-centennial Tournament.

He returned to the United Kingdom to take the Welsh manager's job and had seven and a half seasons in charge during which time Wales were unlucky not to qualify for the final stages of major tournaments. In 1984 he was awarded the MBE for his services to Welsh football.

EUROPEAN CUP WINNERS' CUP

Cardiff City first entered the European Cup Winners' Cup in 1964-65 and after a goalless draw against Esjberg in Denmark, won the return match at Ninian Park with a Peter King goal. In the second round, the Bluebirds drew the holders, Sporting Lisbon of Portugal. The Ninian Park club performed miracles in the first leg in Lisbon, winning 2-1 with goals from Farrell and Tapscott, and though the return leg in Cardiff was goalless, City were through to the quarter-finals in their first European campaign. After trailing 2-0 to Real Zaragoza of Spain, goals from Gareth Williams and Peter King levelled the scores. A crowd of 38,458 saw the second leg at Ninian Park and they went down 1-0 on the night and 3-2 on aggregate. The following year, City were stopped at the first hurdle by the strong Belgian team, Standard Liege but in 1967-68 the Bluebirds embarked on one

Cardiff City 2 SV Hamburg 3
May 1st 1968 - European Cup Winners' Cup Semi Final 2nd leg (Att: 43,070)

of the most glorious chapters in their history.

After beating Shamrock Rovers 3-1 and then the Dutch side NAC Breda 5-2, the club drew Moscow Torpedo in the quarter-finals. Every member of the Torpedo side was a Russian international with Edvard Streltsov, the Russian Player of the Year. City won the first leg at Ninian Park with a Barrie Jones goal just before half-time. Despite sticking defiantly to their task in the second leg in front of 65,000 fans in the Cotton Pickers Stadium in Tashkent, the Bluebirds lost 1-0 and so the tie went to a play-off in Augsberg, West Germany. The Russian side's poor finishing and Cardiff's continued defiance kept the game goalless until Norman Dean scored the winner for City. Cardiff's semi-final opponents were SV Hamburg and with Dean again scoring for City they held the Germans to a 1-1 draw at the Volspark Stadium but City lost the second leg 3-2.

In 1968, goals from Toshack and Bird gave City a two-goal advantage over FC Porto but Pinto the Portuguese club's substitute scored two late goals to make it 2-2. City lost the second leg in Oporto 2-1 to go out in the first round 4-3 on aggregate.

The following season saw Cardiff establish their record away score in the competition when they beat Norwegian team Mjondalen 7-1. In the return at Ninian Park, Sandy Allen headed a hat-trick in a 5-1 victory to give City their record aggregate win of 12-2. They went out in the second round to Turkish side Izmir 3-1 on aggregate.

In 1970-71 City achieved their biggest win in a European tie when they beat P. O. Larnaca of Cyprus 8-0 at Ninian park, later playing out a goal-less draw in the away leg. In the second round, the Bluebirds played some marvellous football to beat Nantes 5-1 at Ninian Park before winning 2-1 in France. In the quarter-finals, a Brian Clark header gave City one of their most memorable victories when Real Madrid were beaten 1-0 in front of a 47,500 Ninian Park crowd. In the return game in the Bernabeu Stadium, City gave their all but went out of the competition 2-1 on aggregate.

In the first round of the 1971-72 competition, both matches against East German side Dynamo Berlin ended 1-1 and so the tie went to a penalty shoot-out. The score stood at 5-4 in favour of the German side when Don Murray blasted his spot-kick high over the crossbar.

In 1973-74, City were knocked out in the first round, losing 2-1 at Sporting Lisbon after the first leg at Ninian Park had ended goalless. There was another early exit for the Bluebirds in 1974-75 as Hungarian side Ferencvaros won 6-1 on aggregate after a superb display of one-touch football at Ninian Park resulted in a 4-1 win for the visitors.

In 1976-77, City beat Swiss Cup holders Servette Geneva in the preliminary round on the away goals rule, before an Adrian Alston goal gave the Bluebirds a 1-0 first round first leg lead over Dynamo Tbilisi. In the return leg, a crowd of 100,000 saw the Russian side win 3-0 to end City's interest in the competition.

The following season saw City's lowest attendance for a European match, 3,631, seeing them play out a goalless draw against FK Austria Memphis before a depleted Bluebirds side lost in Austria to the only goal of the tie.

There was then an 11-year gap before the Ninian Park club were involved in the European Cup Winners' Cup again when in 1988-89 they played Derry City. Following a goalless draw in Ireland, City beat their Irish rivals 4-0 at Ninian Park with Jimmy Gilligan becoming only the second Cardiff City player to score a hat-trick in European competition. The Bluebirds went out of the competition in the second round, losing 6-1 on aggregate to Danish side Aarhus.

City last entered the European Cup Winners' Cup in 1993-94 but went out of the competition in the first round as Standard Liege of Belgium beat them 8-3 on aggregate.

EVANS, JACK

After beginning his career with Wrexham, Jack Evans became Cardiff City's first professional signing when he joined the Bluebirds in 1910. He scored the first goal by a City player at Ninian Park when he netted in the friendly match against Aston Villa.

One of the greatest players in the club's early years, the left-winger scored 52 goals in 170 Southern League games before making his Football League debut in the 5-2 win at Stockport County in the club's inaugural game. After that, Evans became more of a provider than goalscorer and in 1920-21, the club's first season in the League, he provided the crosses for many of Jimmy Gill's goals as the Bluebirds won promotion to the First Division.

A Welsh international, he was a virtual ever-present in City's League side for five seasons before losing his place to George McLachlan who joined the club from Clyde.

The Welsh-speaking Evans played in 395 first team games for Cardiff City before leaving to join Bristol Rovers. At Eastville he teamed up again with Joe Clennell and appeared in a further 65 League games before hanging up his boots.

EVANS, TONY

A former electrician, Tony Evans began his Football League career with Blackpool but never made his mark at Bloomfield Road. He joined Cardiff City in the summer of 1975 and made his debut in a 1-0 win at Brighton and Hove Albion in the third game of the 1975-76 season. That campaign saw him score 31 goals in 57 matches and top the club's League goalscoring charts with 21 strikes as the Bluebirds won promotion to the Second Division. The club also won the Welsh Cup in 1976 with Evans who netted a hat-trick in a 5-0 win over Sully, scoring in both legs of the final against Hereford United.

Tony Evans

The following season, Evans was again the club's leading scorer with 24 goals in 57 games including all four in the 4-4 draw at Bristol Rovers in a League Cup first round second leg tie. In 1977-78, Evans was hampered by a thigh injury and though he returned to first team action in readiness for the 1978-79 campaign, he left Ninian Park at the end of that season to join Birmingham City.

Evans who had scored 62 goals in 153 first team games during his time with the Welsh club, cost the St Andrew's club £120,000 and though an occasional lack of control let him down, he scored 28 goals in 66 League games for Birmingham. He later played for Crystal Palace, Wolverhampton Wanderers, Bolton Wanderers on loan and Swindon Town before leaving the game.

EVER-PRESENTS

There have been 36 Cardiff City players who have been ever-present throughout a Football League season. The greatest number of ever-present seasons by a Bluebirds player is three, a record held by Danny Malloy and Don Murray.

F

FA CUP

In the club's inaugural season of League football, City surprised everybody by reaching the semi-final of the FA Cup. A George Beare goal gave City a 1-0 win at Sunderland in the first round and a place in round two at Brighton and Hove Albion. After a goalless draw at the Goldstone Ground, Arthur Cashmore netted the only goal of the replay to take the Bluebirds into the third round.

A large Welsh contingent travelled to the Dell to see Jimmy Gill score the only goal of a sometimes over-physical contest. City also won the fourth round tie at home to Chelsea by a single goal when Arthur Cashmore fired home from close range.

Facing fellow Second Division club, Wolverhampton Wanderers at Anfield, City played out a goalless draw. Still to concede a goal, City met the Molineux club in the semi-final replay at Old Trafford four days later, but two refereeing decisions went against them and though Fred Keenor pulled a goal back from the penalty-spot, Wolves added a third to win 3-1.

After reaching the quarter-finals in 1921-22 and 1923-24, City went all the way to the final in 1924-25. Facing the eventual champions of the Third Division (North), Darlington in the first round, the Bluebirds won at the third attempt 2-0 after the first two games had been goalless.

In round two, a Len Davies goal was enough to defeat Fulham.

The third round saw Cardiff travel to play Notts County and win 2-0 with goals from Nicholson and Gill. Round four brought the eventual

FA Cup Final - Cardiff City 1 Arsenal 0 - April 23rd 1927
Cardiff City Captain Fred Keenor comes down from the Royal Box with the FA Cup.
Behind him are Billy Hardy (hidden), Jimmy Nelson, Tom Sloan and Sam Irving.

Second Division champions Leicester City to Ninian Park.

The game stood at 1-1 and looked to be heading for a replay when Willie Davies scored the winning goal with the very last kick of the game direct from a corner kick.

In the semi-final, City overcame Blackburn Rovers 3-1 at Meadow Lane with goals from Nicholson, Gill and Beadles. In the final, City faced Sheffield United but a mistake by Harry Wake allowed United's England international winger Tunstall to run on and score the game's only goal.

In 1926-27, the Bluebirds reached Wembley for a second time and created history by becoming the first club to take the Cup out of England when they beat Arsenal 1-0. Goals by Len Davies and Ernie Curtis gave City a 2-1 home win over Aston Villa in the third round before McLachlan and Ferguson scored in a 2-0 win at Darlington in round four.

The fifth round saw City turn in a superb performance against the Cup holders Bolton Wanderers at Burnden Park where a penalty from Hughie Ferguson and a goal from Len Davies, who converted Ferguson's cross, gave the Welsh club a 2-0 win.

A crowd of 70,184 saw City play out a goalless draw against Chelsea at Stamford Bridge in the sixth round but the replay at Ninian Park four days later certainly made up for the drabness of the first meeting. The Bluebirds took an early two-goal lead through Irving and Davies before Farquharson in the City goal saved a penalty.

Just on half-time, the London club did pull a goal back when the ball went through a hole in the netting, though there were many in the ground who thought it had gone wide of the post.

The visitors then equalised within five minutes of the restart but in the 83rd minute City were awarded a penalty and Ferguson struck home the winning goal.

Ferguson scored two goals in the 3-0 semi-final defeat of Reading at Molineux to take the club into their second final. Against all the odds, City beat Arsenal 1-0 with Ferguson being credited with the goal, although film taken from behind the goal shows that the ball last touched the elbow of Arsenal 'keeper Lewis before crossing the line.

Since then, the club's best performance has been to reach the fifth round, the last time against Luton in 1994.

The Bluebirds biggest victory in the FA Cup is 8-0 against Enfield in the first round of the 1931-32 competition, whilst the club's biggest defeat is 6-1 by Aston Villa in the third round of the 1928-29 competition.

FA CUP FINALS
Cardiff City have appeared in two FA Cup Finals.

1925   Cardiff City 0 Sheffield United 1

The only goal of the game was scored after 32 minutes by Sheffield United outside-left Tunstall. Cardiff half-back Harry Wake was caught in possession by the Blades' winger who ran and shot past Tom Farquharson in the City goal. The Bluebirds were very disappointing and in a post-match statement, City captain Fred Keenor apologised for their performance and absolved Wake of causing the club's downfall. He also vowed that City would return to Wembley and win the trophy !

The Cardiff City side was: T.Farquharson; J.Nelson; J.Blair; H.Wake; F.Keenor; W.Hardy; W.Davies; J.Gill; J.Nicholson; H.Beadles and J.Evans.

1927   Cardiff City 1 Arsenal 0

Harry Wake who was eager to make amends after his costly mistake two years earlier, was injured just one week before the final and had to sit this one out. The match was never a classic and half-time arrived with the game goalless. The only goal of what was a fairly dour encounter came in the 74th minute. Cardiff centre-forward Hughie Ferguson shot from the edge of the penalty area and Arsenal's Welsh international 'keeper Dan Lewis went down to his left to gather the ball. With Len Davies following up, the Arsenal goalkeeper who was practically on all-fours, shot out his left arm to try and reach the loose ball but the next thing the spectators saw was the ball trickling over the line to give Cardiff the honour of being the first club in the history of the game to take the Cup out of England.

The Cardiff City side was: T.Farquharson; J.Nelson; T.Watson; F.Keenor; T.Sloan; W.Hardy; E.Curtis; S.Irving; H.Ferguson; L.Davies and G.McLachlan.

FARQUHARSON, TOM
Without doubt the greatest goalkeeper in the history of the club, Dublin-born Tom Farquharson joined Cardiff City from Abertillery and made his debut in a 3-1 home win over Manchester United on the final day of the

1921-22 season. The following season he shared the goalkeeping duties with Ben Davies but in 1923-24 he became the club's first-choice 'keeper, a position he held for the next 12 seasons. Also in 1923-24 he won the first of seven caps for Northern Ireland when he played against Scotland. Six seasons later he won the first of four caps for the Republic of Ireland.

He was in goal when City lost 1-0 to Sheffield United in the FA Cup Final and when they beat Arsenal, also at Wembley in 1927.

The law that made sure that the goalkeepers' feet remained on the goal-line when a penalty-kick was being taken is down to the antics of Tom Farquharson. He would quite often advance from the back of the net as the penalty-taker came in to take the kick !

Farquharson went on to play in 521 first team games for Cardiff City, his last appearance for the Welsh club being in a 4-0 defeat at Bristol City on the final day of the 1934-35 season.

FATHER AND SON

One of the most notable father and son combinations is that of Jimmy and Doug Blair. Jimmy was a Scottish international full-back who began his career with Clyde before joining Sheffield Wednesday in 1914. Unfortunately his progress at Hillsborough was interrupted by the First World War, but after the hostilities had ended he refused to return to Sheffield from Scotland. Eventually he was persuaded to do so but in November 1920 he joined Cardiff for a fee of £3,500. Over the next six years he appeared in 175 League games and was a member of the Cardiff side which lost 1-0 to Sheffield United in the FA Cup Final of 1925.

His son Doug became one of the Bluebirds' greatest players in the immediate post-war years. He scored 28 goals in 201 League appearances and was an important member of the Cardiff side which won promotion to the First Division in 1951-52.

FERGUSON, HUGHIE

Motherwell-born centre-forward Hughie Ferguson began his career with his home-town club in 1916. Over the next nine years the prolific Ferguson scored a remarkable 362 goals for the Scottish club.

He joined Cardiff City in November 1925 when the Welsh club paid £5,000 for his services and at the same time, George McLachlan also arrived at Ninian Park at a cost of £2,000. Ferguson scored one of City's goals on his debut in a 5-2 home win over Leicester City and ended the season with 19 goals in 26 games including a hat-trick in a 4-2 win at Notts

County. In 1926-27 he established a new club scoring record with 26 goals in 39 games including eight doubles. Also that season he netted six FA Cup goals including being credited with the winning goal in the Wembley final win over Arsenal. The following season he scored 18 goals in 32 games and scored both goals in the Welsh Cup Final when the Bluebirds beat Bangor City 2-0. In 1928-29 when the club were relegated from the First Division, Ferguson was injured for most of the season but still managed 14 goals including five in a 7-0 home win over Burnley.

He had scored 92 goals in 139 games for the Ninian Park club when Dundee made an offer that City could not refuse, but his transfer was to end in tragedy.

Unable to shake off an injury, he found it difficult to find the net and was heckled by the Dundee supporters who expected more from him. Hughie Ferguson was a sensitive person and on 9 January 1930, the player who had put the Bluebirds into football history, gassed himself after a training session at Dens Park.

FESTIVAL OF BRITAIN
The Festival of Britain was held in 1951, and to celebrate the event, the majority of Football League sides played matches against foreign touring sides. On 9 May 1951, a crowd of 10,000 saw City draw 2-2 with Dutch side Eindhoven with the Bluebirds' goals being scored by Mike Tiddy and Wilf Grant.

FIRE
The Main Stand at Ninian Park was completely burned to the ground in the early hours of Monday 18 January 1937. It is thought that the fire was caused by burglars who were after the takings from the third round FA Cup match against Grimsby Town the previous Saturday which the Bluebirds lost 3-1 in front of a 36,245 crowd.

FIRST DIVISION
The Bluebirds have had three spells in the First Division. Though they failed to win any of the first six matches in their first season in the top flight, 1921-22, they recovered to finish fourth. After finishing ninth the following season, City missed winning the League Championship in 1923-24 by the narrowest of margins. Len Davies missed a late penalty in the last match of the season at Birmingham that would have given Cardiff the title. City only took one point from the five matches played in March and

it cost them dear. City spent eight seasons in the First Division before being relegated in 1928-29 despite conceding fewer goals than any First Division club !

The club had to wait until 1952-53 for their next spell in the top flight. They ended the campaign in mid-table despite going five consecutive matches at the turn of the year without scoring a goal. In 1955-56, Wolverhampton Wanderers beat the Bluebirds 9-1 at Ninian Park to equal the record First Division away score. The following season, City were relegated after a 2-1 win at West Bromwich Albion was their only success in the last 14 games of the season.

The club's last spell in the First Division lasted two seasons. In 1960-61 City finished 15th but managed to complete the 'double' over League champions Burnley, winning 2-1 both at Ninian Park and Turf Moor. The following season of 1961-62 was Cardiff's last in the top flight, their fate being sealed in an 8-3 defeat at Everton in the penultimate game of the season.

FIRST LEAGUE MATCH
Following their successful application to the Second Division of the Football League, Cardiff City's opening match was at Edgeley Park on 28 August 1920 when they faced Stockport County, former employers of Bluebirds' manager Fred Stewart.

Stockport took an early lead through Pat Norris, but after 15 minutes City drew level when Jimmy Gill scored the club's first goal in League football. The Cardiff forward scored his and Cardiff's second on the half-hour and then further goals from Billy Grimshaw, Fred Keenor and Jack Evans took the score to five before County's Charles Danskin grabbed a late consolation goal from the penalty spot.

The Cardiff City side of that historic day was:
J.Kneeshaw; R.C.Brittan; A.Layton; W.Hardy; E.E.Smith; F.Keenor;
W.Grimshaw; J.Gill; A.Cashmore; W.West and J.Evans.

FIRST MATCH
In 1899-1900, the club's first season, they only played friendly matches. The first of these saw the newly formed team lose 9-1 to Barry West End!

FLOODLIGHTS
The Ninian Park floodlights were belatedly installed and were opened in August 1960 in a match against Sheffield Wednesday.

FOOTBALL LEAGUE CUP

With the exception of 1965-66 when the club reached the semi-finals, the Bluebirds have failed to make much impact upon the Football League Cup (later Milk Cup, Littlewoods Cup, Rumbelows Cup and Coca Cola Cup).

The club's first game in the competition was on 3 October 1960 when they won 4-3 against Middlesbrough at Ayresome Park with Walsh, Donnelly, Hudson and Edwards the City scorers. In the second round at Ninian Park, City lost 4-0 to Burnley for whom Gordon Harris netted a hat-trick.

In that 1965-66 season, City drew their first match, a second round tie at Crewe Alexandra 1-1 before two goals from Peter King helped them to a 3-0 win in the replay. King was on the scoresheet again in round three as Portsmouth were beaten 2-0, whilst in the next round, teenage scoring sensation George Johnston netted a hat-trick in a 5-1 defeat of Reading. Ipswich Town were beaten 2-1 in the fifth round before City faced First Division West Ham United in the two-legged semi-final. Despite two goals from George Andrews, City lost the first leg at Upton Park 5-2 and then went down 5-1 at home to the London club to go out 10-3 on aggregate !

When the Bluebirds faced Bristol Rovers at Eastville in a first round second leg tie in 1976-77, Tony Evans became the first City player to score four goals in the competition as the Welsh club drew 4-4 to go through on aggregate 6-5.

Another exciting game in the League Cup occurred on 26 August 1986 when City entertained Plymouth Argyle. The visitors raced into a two-goal lead before Nigel Vaughan reduced the arrears, but then Argyle added two more against the run of play to go in at half-time 4-1 up. The Bluebirds then scored two goals in three minutes at the start of the second half courtesy of Rob Turner and Nigel Vaughan and then captain Terry Boyle equalised. With both teams going all-out for the winner, it was City in the shape of Paul Wheeler who scored the all important goal in the 83rd minute to complete a superb fight back by the Ninian Park club. Sadly, only 2,503 saw the game !

FORD, MIKE

The son of Tony Ford who was a full-back with both Bristol clubs, he served his apprentice ship with Leicester City before becoming a full-time professional at the age of 18. After being released by the Filbert Street club, he moved into the Western League with Devizes Town but within a matter of months he joined Cardiff City and made his debut in a 1-1 draw at Leeds United.

He proved himself to be a fine utility player at Ninian Park, appearing at full-back, central defence and midfield. In the club's promotion-winning season of 1987-88 he scored seven goals in 45 appearances and was one of the mainstays of the Bluebirds team. Ford went on to score 13 goals in 145 League games for Cardiff before leaving the club to join Oxford United in the 1988 close season. He remained there for 10 years and rejoined City in the summer of 1998.

FORD, TREVOR

Welsh international Trevor Ford chose to start his League career with his home-town club of Swansea in 1941, despite a number of other clubs, including Cardiff City, wanting to sign him. After scoring 44 goals in 41 games for the Swans in the 1945-46 season and nine in the opening six games of the following campaign, Ford left the Vetch Field to join Aston Villa for a fee of £10,000.

He made his Villa debut in a 2-0 win at Highbury in January 1947 and in nine games that season, he scored nine goals. In terms of goals scored, his best seasons were 1947-48 and 1949-50 when he netted 18 in each campaign, although on 27 December 1948 he scored four goals as Villa beat Wolves 5-1. In October 1950, Ford left Villa Park after scoring 61 goals in 128 appearances and signed for Sunderland for £30,000. In three years at Roker Park, Ford scored 67 goals in 108 games before Cardiff paid what was then their record fee of £30,000 to bring him to Ninian Park.

After making his debut in a 2-1 defeat at Sheffield Wednesday in December 1953, Ford soon became a firm favourite with the Cardiff supporters. Though not as prolific a scorer as in his early playing days, he did net four goals in two Welsh Cup games as Pembroke Borough were beaten 7-0 in 1954-55 and 9-0 in 1955-56. He had scored 59 goals in 119 outings for the Bluebirds when in 1955 he fell out with Trevor Morris following the City manager's decision to play him at inside-right.

After leaving Ninian Park, Ford was banned *sine die* by the Football League following his revelations about Sunderland Football Club in his autobiography 'I lead the attack'. Between 1957 and 1960 he played in Holland with PSV Eindhoven. After a brief spell with Newport County, Ford ended his playing career with non-League Romford.

FORMATION

The establishment of a first-class professional football club in a rugby stronghold such as Cardiff is due to the members of the Riverside club formed in 1899 out of a cricket club of that name. The original idea was to form a football team in order to keep all the cricketers fit during the winter months. After a disappointing turn out at the inaugural meeting, the idea was scotched but when a second meeting was arranged there was a much better response and the Riverside AFC was formed with Bartley Wilson its first secretary.

FOURTH DIVISION

Cardiff City have had two spells in the Fourth Division. Their first match in the League's basement was at Hartlepool United on 23 August 1986 where a Rob Turner goal gave them a 1-1 draw. It was a mixed season for the Bluebirds, having tasted defeat just once in their opening nine matches, they later failed to win a League match at Ninian Park in the period 26 December - 11 April, drawing seven and losing three of the ten games and had to settle for 13th position.

The following season, Jimmy Gilligan bought from Lincoln City for £17,500 scored 20 League goals as City ended the season with five successive wins and promotion to the Third Division as runners-up to Wolverhampton Wanderers. For the record, the Bluebirds did the 'double' over the Molineux club, winning 3-2 at Ninian Park and 4-1 away from home.

The club's second spell in the Fourth Division began in 1990-91. City were undefeated in their first seven matches, though five of these were drawn. They hovered around mid-table for most of the season and there were hopes that they could reach the play-offs but after failing to win any of their last eight games, they had to settle for 13th place.

In 1991-92 City moved up four places but were beaten 5-0 at home by Maidstone United. Following reorganisation the Bluebirds were in the 'new' Third Division for the 1992-93 season when they won the Championship with 83 points. Two years later they returned to the League's basement where they have been for the last three seasons, winning a play-off place in 1996-97.

FREIGHT ROVER TROPHY

The Freight Rover Trophy replaced the initial Associate Members Cup for the 1984-85 season, though it was the following season before the Bluebirds first participated. Grouped with Newport County and Swansea City, Cardiff failed to make the knockout stages, losing both matches 1-0 and 2-0 respectively. The 1986-87 season was no different with City again losing both group matches and again failing to score a goal, losing 1-0 at home to Wolverhampton Wanderers and by the same scoreline at Bournemouth.

G

GALBRAITH, JOHN

Scottish half-back John Galbraith played his early football with Vale of Leven before joining Clapton Orient in 1921. He spent ten seasons with the London club, appearing in 280 games before moving to Ninian Park in February 1931.

His first game for the Bluebirds was in a 1-0 home defeat by Bristol City and though he played in 11 of the club's last 14 games in that 1930-31 season, he couldn't prevent the club being relegated from the Second Division. Over the next four seasons, Galbraith missed very few matches and in 1933-34 when the club finished bottom of the Second Division and had to seek re-election he scored his first League goal in a 5-1 defeat at home to Bristol City.

Galbraith played in 157 first team games for City before leaving Ninian Park to manage Milford United. In 1938 he returned to his beloved Orient as coach.

GIBBINS, ROGER

After playing his early football with Tottenham Hotspur, the Enfield-born midfielder joined Oxford United in the summer of 1975 and made his League debut for the Manor Ground club. After just one season he moved to Norwich City where he scored 12 goals in 48 League games before going to play in America for the New England Teamen. He returned to England in September 1979 and joined Cambridge United. A regular member of the side, he spent three seasons at the Abbey Stadium, scoring 12 goals in his 100 League outings.

At the end of the 1981-82 season he was given a free transfer and joined Cardiff City, making his debut in a 2-1 home defeat by Wrexham on the opening day of the 1982-83 season. That season he was the club's only ever-present and scored eight League goals as the Bluebirds won promotion. He was ever-present again in 1983-84 and played in 91 consecutive League matches from his debut. He had appeared in 160 first team games when he joined Swansea City in exchange for Chris Marustik in October 1985.

He had just one season at Vetch Field before joining Newport County but when the Somerton Park club lost their League status he moved to Torquay United. In March 1989 he returned to Ninian Park for a second spell and took his Cardiff career record to 31 goals in 271 games before leaving to join Newport AFC at the end of the 1990-91 season.

Roger Gibbins

GIBSON, IAN

Ian Gibson was just 15 years old when he made his League debut for Accrington Stanley but after scoring three goals in nine games for the Peel Park club, he was transferred to Bradford Park Avenue, another club that was to lose its League status. Gibson spent two years at Park Avenue, scoring 18 goals in 88 League games before Middlesbrough paid £30,000 for his services in March 1962.

A former Scottish Schoolboy international, he was capped at Under-23 level whilst at Ayresome Park but could do nothing to halt Boro's slide into the Third Division. He had scored 44 goals in 168 games for the north-east club when Coventry City paid £40,000 to take Gibson to Highfield Road. He scored 13 goals in 93 League games for the Sky Blues and helped them win promotion to the First Division.

He joined Cardiff City in the summer of 1970 for a fee of £35,000 and made his debut in a 1-0 win at Leicester City on the opening day of the 1970-71 season. That season he scored six goals in 40 League games but provided many more for Clark, Toshack and Warboys. In that campaign, he scored two goals in City's 3-1 Welsh Cup Final win over Wrexham.

In 1971-72 he again missed just two games but this time his season was spent in helping the club avoid relegation to the Third Division. Gibson had scored 18 goals in 118 games before leaving City in October 1972 to join Bournemouth in a £100,000 deal.

Within months of his arrival at Dean Court he was forced to quit the game through injury.

GILES, DAVID

A much-travelled player, David Giles was a Welsh Schoolboy international when he joined Cardiff City. He played his first game for the club in a goalless draw at Nottingham Forest in February 1975. He had played in 70 first team games, scoring 10 goals when in December 1978, Wrexham paid £20,000 to take him to the Racecourse Ground. In two seasons with the Robins he played in 48 games before Swansea City paid £40,000 for his services.

In two years at the Vetch Field, he won nine of his 12 Welsh international caps and helped the Swans win promotion to the First Division.

After a short loan spell with Orient, Giles joined Crystal Palace, where his form was such that he continued to play for his country. After Selhurst Park he had two months at Birmingham City without playing a game and then he moved to Newport County. When the Somerton Park club released him, he returned to Cardiff in September 1985 and took his total of City first team appearances to 134 before leaving to play part-time football for Barry Town in the Welsh League.

GILL, JIMMY

The scorer of Cardiff City's first goal in League football, inside-right Jimmy Gill began his career with his home-town club Sheffield Wednesday but with the Yorkshire club experiencing financial difficulties he was sold to Cardiff City for £750 in 1920.

He scored twice on his debut as the Bluebirds won 5-2 at Stockport County in what was the club's first-ever League match. He ended the season as City's leading scorer with 19 League goals as the club won promotion to the First Division as runners-up to Birmingham. In 1921-22 he again topped the club's League goalscoring charts with 20 goals, including five 'doubles'. Also that season he won a Welsh Cup winners' medal, scoring in the final in a 2-0 win over Ton Pentre.

The following season, Gill scored 17 League goals including a hat-trick in a 5-0 home win over Blackburn Rovers. The Bluebirds retained the Welsh Cup and as well as scoring in the final again in a 3-2 win over Aberdare Athletic, he netted two hat-tricks in the earlier rounds of the competition as Rhymney were beaten 7-0 and Oswestry 10-0.

He continued to find the net in 1923-24 and notched his second League hat-trick in a 4-0 home win over Arsenal. He was in the City team that lost 1-0 to Sheffield United in the FA Cup Final of 1925 but the following year he left Ninian Park to play for Blackpool.

Gill was without doubt one of the club's greatest players, scoring 103 goals in 220 first team games. After a short stay at Bloomfield Road he played for Derby County before ending his career with Crystal Palace.

GILLIGAN, JIMMY

A former England Youth international, Jimmy Gilligan began his career with Watford but in six years at Vicarage Road, the bustling centre-forward scored just six goals in 27 League appearances. After a loan spell at Lincoln, he joined Grimsby Town for £100,000 but within twelve months he had left Blundell Park to sign for Swindon Town for £40,000. Gilligan was soon on the move again, this time to Lincoln City after a loan spell in South Wales with Newport County. When the Sincil Bank club lost their League status in 1987, Gilligan moved to Cardiff City for what proved a bargain fee of £17,500.

He scored City's goal on his debut in a 1-1 draw at home to Leyton

Orient and ended the season as the club's top scorer with 20 League goals as the Bluebirds won promotion to the Third Division. One of two ever-presents in that 1987-88 season, he also won a Welsh Cup winners' medal, scoring the second goal in a 2-0 win over Wrexham. He was ever-present again the following season and the club's top scorer with 14 League goals and in the European Cup Winners' Cup netted a hat-trick in a 4-0 home win over Derry City. Early the following season, after scoring 49 goals in 131 first team games, he followed former City manager Frank Burrows to Portsmouth before returning to South Wales to end his League career with Swansea City where once again he scored regularly.

GOAL AVERAGE

Cardiff City were twice deprived of championship successes in Divisions One and Two on goal average. In 1920-21 when they finished second to Birmingham, their average was 1.843 compared with Birmingham's 2.078. In 1923-24 they lost the Division One title to Huddersfield Town whose 1.818 was marginally better than Cardiff's 1.794.

Had goal difference been in operation at the time, City would not have won Division Two in 1920-21 but they would have overtaken Huddersfield Town in 1923-24. Although both teams had identical figures of +27 Cardiff would have won the title by scoring one more goal than their rivals.

GOALKEEPERS

Cardiff City FC has almost always been extremely well served by its goalkeepers and most of them have been highly popular with the supporters.

The club's first outstanding 'keeper was Jack Kneeshaw who was a virtual ever-present during City's Southern League days. He played 34 League games for the club before joining City's coaching staff.

Tom Farquharson is probably the greatest goalkeeper ever to play for Cardiff City. An Irish international, he was in goal when City won the FA Cup in 1927 and played in 445 League games for the Ninian Park club.

Danny Canning was in Cardiff's goal when they won the Third Division (South) championship in 1946-47 and played in 78 games from his debut before joining Swansea Town, whom he also helped to promotion. Graham Vearncombe appeared in 208 League games for the Bluebirds yet only won two full caps for Wales, when his performances merited more.

Irish Amateur international Bill Irwin turned in some memorable displays in his 180 League games for the club, though he has the unenviable distinction of being the first City goalkeeper to be sent off when he was dismissed in the Welsh Cup tie against Oswestry in February 1974.

Ron Healey, the former Manchester City 'keeper was in direct competition to Irwin at this time. When Irwin left, Healey was the club's first choice for five years, his performances earning him two full caps for the Republic of Ireland.

The club have also had international 'keepers in Andy Dibble and George Wood, whilst the club's present custodian at the time of writing is Jon Hallworth.

GOALS

The most goals Cardiff City have ever scored in one game was their 16-0 victory against Knighton Town in a Welsh Cup fifth round tie at Ninian Park on 28 January 1961. Derek Tapscott scored six, Graham Moore four, Brian Walsh and Peter Donnelly two apiece and Derek Hogg and Danny Malloy one goal each.

In the League, City beat Thames Association 9-2 on 6 February 1932 with Walter Robbins scoring five of the goals.

GOALS - CAREER BEST

The highest goalscorer in the club's history is Len Davies who between season 1920-21 and the end of 1930-31 had netted 184 goals for the club.

These comprised of 128 in the Football League, 19 in the FA Cup, 35 in the Welsh Cup and one in the FA Charity Shield match against Corinthians.

GOALS - INDIVIDUAL

There are three instances of players scoring five goals in a League game for Cardiff City. The first was Hughie Ferguson who netted five in City's 7-0 home win over Burnley on 1 September 1928. Despite his goalscoring exploits, the Bluebirds finished bottom of the First Division and were relegated. Walter Robbins hit five in the club's record League win on 6 February 1932 when Thames Association were beaten 9-2. The last player to score five goals in a League game was Jim Henderson on 22 April 1933 when Northampton Town were defeated 6-0. Just 7,000 saw his achievement.

There is an instance of a Cardiff player scoring six goals in a match and that came on 28 January 1961 when Knighton Town were beaten 16-0 in a fifth round Welsh Cup tie. The man who scored six of City's goals that day was former Arsenal and Wales' centre-forward, Derek Tapscott.

GOALS - SEASON

The club's highest League goalscorer in any one season remains Stan Richards who scored 30 League goals as Cardiff finished the 1946-47 campaign as champions of the Third Division (South). The season's highest tally for all matches is the 31 goals achieved by John Toshack in 1968-69. The Welsh international forward scored 22 in the League, seven in the Welsh Cup and two in the European Cup Winners' Cup.

GOODFELLOW, JIMMY

Midfielder Jimmy Goodfellow played for Crook Town and Bishop Auckland before joining Port Vale in the summer of 1966. After three seasons at Vale Park in which he scored 11 goals in 95 League and Cup games, he joined Workington. He played in 199 League games for the Cumbrian club before playing for Rotherham United and Stockport County.

After his playing days were over he became the trainer and then the coach of Newport County. When Len Ashurst moved to Ninian Park in 1982, Goodfellow followed him as his assistant. When Ashurst left in 1984, he had a short period officially in charge of the club at the start of the 1984-85 season. Yet, with little help from the club's board of directors, he was eventually replaced by Alan Durban.

He then had a spell as physiotherapist at Sunderland before returning to Ninian Park in a similar capacity.

GRANT, WILF

Ashington-born Wilf Grant began his Football League career with Southampton in 1946 and after scoring 11 goals in 61 League games he joined Cardiff City. He made his debut in a 1-0 home win over Coventry City in March 1950 and played in the remaining 12 games of the season. After playing at both outside and inside-right at the beginning of the 1950-51 season, he was switched to centre-forward following the signing of Mike Tiddy from Torquay, with devastating results.

City finished third in Division Two and Grant netted 14 League goals from just 25 games in the centre-forward position including a hat-trick in a 5-2 home win over Grimsby Town.

When the club were promoted to the First Division the following season, Grant was the club's only ever-present and top scored with 26 League goals. In the top flight he continued to find the net and his form won him an England 'B' cap. He went on to score 73 goals in 169 first team games for the Bluebirds before leaving the club to join Ipswich Town in October 1954.

In his second season at Portman Road he scored 16 goals in 35 games including hat-tricks in two successive games - Millwall (Home 6-2) and Reading (Away 5-1). He scored 22 goals in 78 League games for Ipswich including another hat-trick against Millwall later in that 1955-56 season.

When his playing days were over, he returned to Ninian Park as a member of the club's coaching staff.

GRAPES, STEVE

Steve Grapes began his League career with his home-town club, Norwich City in 1970, but after six seasons with the Carrow Road club, in which he made just 41 League appearances and a loan spell at Bournemouth, he signed for Cardiff City for a fee of £7,000.

He made his debut for the Bluebirds in a goalless draw at Burnley in December 1976 and went on to appear in 22 games, helping the club avoid relegation to the Third Division. When he arrived at Ninian Park he was an orthodox winger but later into his City career, he switched to inside-forward. Though he only scored seven goals in his 167 first team outings, he laid on plenty of chances for the team's strikers. He was released at the end of the 1981-82 season and joined Torquay United where he played in 31 League games for the Devon club before returning to South Wales to play out his career with Merthyr Tydfil.

GRIFFITH, COHEN

The Bluebirds paid Kettering Town £60,000 for the services of Cohen Griffith in October 1989 and he scored after just 19 minutes of his first team

Cohen Griffith

debut as City won 3-2 at Huddersfield Town. He ended the season with 10 goals in 38 League games but City were relegated. He continued to find the back of the net the following season and scored in each of the club's four Football League Cup games. In 1991-92 he was moved into more of a defensive midfield role and after helping the club win promotion the following season, went on to score 39 goals in 234 League games before being given a free transfer at the end of the 1994-95 season.

GRIMSHAW, BILLY
After playing reserve team football with his home-town club, Burnley, inside-right Billy Grimshaw joined Bradford City in 1912 and was an important member of their League side up until the outbreak of the First World War. At the end of the hostilities, he joined Cardiff City for £1,000 and played his first game in a 2-0 defeat at Reading on the opening day of the 1919-20 Southern League season. He ended that season, the club's last in that competition, with 14 goals in 32 appearances.

He scored on his League debut in the club's inaugural game at Stockport County which the Bluebirds won 5-2. Grimshaw, who was a virtual ever-present over the next three seasons of League football, switched to the right-wing after Jimmy Gill had joined the club from Sheffield Wednesday. His performances in his new position earned him selection for the Football League XI.

After Dennis Lawson, the St Mirren winger had signed for the club, Grimshaw lost his form and his place and having scored 33 goals in 158 games for City, left to continue his League career with Sunderland.

GUEST PLAYERS
The 'guest' system was used by all clubs during the two wars. Although at times it was abused almost beyond belief (in that some sides that opposed the Bluebirds had ten or 11 'guests'!) it normally worked sensibly and effectively to the benefit of players, clubs and supporters alike. The most distinguished players to 'guest' for Cardiff City have been Raich Carter (Sunderland and England), Bill Shankly (Preston North End and Scotland), Cliff Britton (Everton and England) and Johnny Carey (Manchester United and Ireland).

H

HANSBURY, ROGER

Goalkeeper Roger Hansbury began his League career at Norwich City but took a long time to establish himself due to the consistency of Kevin Keelan. When Keelan finally retired, Hansbury's career was disrupted by a broken leg !

Roger Hansbury

Whilst at Carrow Road he spent a loan spell at Cambridge United, helping them win promotion from Division Three in 1977-78. After leaving Norwich he spent a couple of seasons with Eastern Athletic in Hong Kong before joining Burnley.

An ever-present in his first season at Turf Moor, he lost his place in 1984-85 and joined Cambridge again. In March 1986 he moved to Birmingham City as cover for David Seaman, but stepped up when the future England 'keeper moved on to Queen's Park Rangers. Hansbury later drifted around the League completing loan spells at numerous clubs before signing for Cardiff City, his last League club.

He made his debut on 13 October 1989 in a 1-1 home draw against Chester City and though he turned in a number of outstanding displays, he couldn't prevent the Bluebirds being relegated.

In 1990-91 he was the club's only ever-present but then shared the goalkeeping duties with Gavin Ward the following season before leaving Ninian Park after appearing in 99 League games.

HARDY, BILLY

After beginning his career with his home-town club Bedlington United in 1910, left-half Billy Hardy went to play Scottish League football with Heart of Midlothian before returning to England to play for Stockport County.

Hardy arrived at Ninian Park for the start of the club's 1911-12 Southern League season and played his first game for the club in a 3-1 home win over Kettering Town on the opening day of the season. He was a virtual ever-present in City's Southern League days, appearing in 144 matches before the club attained Football League status in 1920.

He made his League debut in the club's first-ever game in the competition, starring in the 5-2 win at Stockport County. He was the club's only ever-present in that 1920-21 season as they won promotion to the First Division. Hardy appeared in both of City's FA Cup Finals and it was often thought that he was only denied an international cap because he was with a Welsh club. He was selected to represent the Football League XI in 1927-28.

Not including wartime games and friendlies, Billy Hardy appeared in a phenomenal 585 first team games for Cardiff City, a total which included 353 Football League matches. His last game in Cardiff colours came at the age of 41 in a 1-0 home win over Gillingham on 28 March 1932.

After leaving Ninian Park at the end of that season, he managed Bradford Park Avenue for four seasons before later working as a chief scout for the Yorkshire club.

HARRINGTON, ALAN

Alan Harrington joined his home-town club, Cardiff City from Cardiff Nomads in October 1951 but he had to wait until midway through the 1952-53 season before being given a chance in the first team. Playing at wing-half he made an impressive debut in a goalless draw at home to Tottenham Hotspur. He went on to make 10 League appearances that season and in his first six matches for the Bluebirds, the opposition failed to score. It was 1954-55 before he established himself as a first team regular and with the exception of missing the entire 1963-64 season with a broken leg, he was a virtual ever-present in the City side for the next 12 seasons.

He was capped at full international by Wales 11 times winning his first cap against Northern Ireland in 1956.

He had played in 405 first team games for the Ninian Park club when he was forced to give the game up following another broken leg in a 1-1 draw at Leyton Orient in January 1966.

HARRIS, BRIAN

Brian Harris joined Everton from Port Sunlight and after making his debut in a 1-0 win at Burnley in August 1955, went on to play in every position except goalkeeper for the Blues' first team. He appeared in 358 League and Cup games, winning a League Championship medal in 1962-63 and an FA Cup winners' medal in 1966 when he was one of Everton's star players in the 3-2 win over Sheffield Wednesday. Best remembered as a defensive wing-half, he was a great favourite with the Goodison crowd. It came as a great surprise in October 1966 when he was allowed to join Cardiff City for £15,000.

He made his debut for the Bluebirds in a 7-1 defeat at Plymouth Argyle, the first of 149 League appearances Harris made for the Ninian Park club. In 1967-68 he played in all nine of the club's European Cup Winners' Cup games when they just missed out on reaching the final. Harris left Cardiff in the summer of 1971 to become player-manager of Newport County. He made 85 appearances for the Somerton Park club and almost led them to promotion in 1972 but he later resigned his post after a disagreement with the board over finances. Harris later returned to Ninian Park as assistant-manager to Richie Morgan, a post he held for two years.

HARRIS, FRANK

Birmingham-born Frank Harris began his career with Bromsgrove before joining Cardiff City in 1928. When he arrived at Ninian Park, Harris was an inside-forward but was soon converted to wing-half where over the next five seasons he was to prove one of the club's most consistent players.

He played his first game for the Bluebirds in a 1-0 defeat at Aston Villa on 29 September 1928 but scored on his home debut the following week as the Welsh club lost 2-1 to Leicester City. In his first three seasons at Ninian Park he was hampered by a series of niggling injuries, but in 1931-32 he missed just two games - one of which was a 5-1 defeat at Reading - as the Bluebirds finished ninth in the Third Division (South).

He had scored 13 goals in 148 games for City when he was rather surprisingly allowed to leave the club and join Charlton Athletic. At The Valley, Harris was instrumental in the club winning successive promotions from the Third Division (South) to the First Division.

HAT-TRICK HEROES

Cardiff City players have netted 53 hat-tricks in Football League games with Walter Robbins, Jim McCambridge, Albert Keating and Derek Tapscott leading the way with three each.

The last hat-trick hero in a League game for the Bluebirds was Andy Saville against Scunthorpe United on 28 February 1998 in a match which City drew 3-3.

The only Cardiff player to score a hat-trick on his debut for the club was Neil O'Halloran on 10 December 1955 when he scored all City's goals in a 3-1 win over Charlton Athletic at Ninian park.

Though there haven't been any occasions in Football League games when two Cardiff players have scored hat-tricks in the same match, there have been four in the Welsh Cup. The first occurred on 14 March 1923 when Len Davies and Jimmy Gill netted three goals apiece in a 10-0 win over Oswestry Town. On 8 February 1956, Trevor Ford scored four goals and Gerry Hitchens three in a 9-0 fifth round replay win over Pembroke Borough. When Knighton Town were thrashed 16-0 on 28 January 1961, Derek Tapscott scored a double hat-trick and Graham Moore four of the goals. The last occasion this feat was achieved was in the 8-0 defeat of Ebbw Vale on 16 January 1968 when John Toshack and Ronnie Bird both netted three goals.

Other hat-trick heroes include Ivor Allchurch who hit a hat-trick against his former club Swansea Town in a 5-0 win on 6 April 1965 and Sandy Allan who scored a headed hat-trick in the 5-1 defeat of Mjondalen in the European Cup Winners' Cup competition of 1969-70.

Although 36 players have scored Football League hat-tricks for the Bluebirds, it is surprising to find that Brian Clark, who scored 79 League goals for City, somehow failed to register a League hat-trick for the club.

On 2 September 1985 when Trevor Senior scored a hat-trick for Reading against Cardiff at Ninian Park, he was refused the gift of the ball by City manager Alan Durban who said he could have it for £40!

HEALEY, RON

Goalkeeper Ron Healey started his career with Manchester City where for most of his time at Maine Road, he was understudy to Joe Corrigan. He had made 40 first team appearances and had loan spells at Coventry City and Preston North End before joining Cardiff City in March 1974.

He made his debut for the Bluebirds in a 2-2 draw at West Bromwich Albion and in the last seven games of the season, his performances between the posts saw City lose just one of those games and so avoid the drop into the Third Division. The following season he found himself in the shadow of Bill Irwin but in the club's promotion-winning season of 1975-76 he played in 33 of the games, keeping eight clean sheets in the last nine games of the season. Over the next six seasons, Healey was the club's first-choice 'keeper and went on to play in 267 games until injury ended his career in 1982.

The Manchester-born 'keeper's consistency during his stay at Ninian Park saw him win two caps at full international level for the Republic of Ireland.

Ron Healey

HEMMERMAN, JEFF

A forward who made his League debut for his home-town club of Hull City, he had a loan spell with Scunthorpe United before joining Port Vale. Given a free transfer, he joined Portsmouth in the summer of 1978 and scored twice on his Pompey debut in a 5-3 defeat at York City. Two games later, he netted a hat-trick as Crewe were beaten 3-0. He ended that season as the club's top scorer with 16 League and Cup goals and in 1979-80 scored 13 League goals as the Fratton Park club won promotion to the Third Division. At the end of the 1981-82 season he was allowed to leave Portsmouth where he had scored 45 goals in 138 games and he joined Cardiff City.

He was the club's leading scorer in 1982-83 with 22 League goals as the Bluebirds won promotion to the Second Division. Sadly he damaged knee ligaments in the club's final game of the season at Bristol Rovers and though he tried a comeback the following season, it was to no avail and after training as a physiotherapist, he helped out at Ninian Park before setting up his own practice in Newport.

HENDERSON, JIM

Jim Henderson joined the Bluebirds from the then Scottish League club, St Bernards of Edinburgh and scored on his debut in a 2-1 home win over Aldershot on 4 February 1933. Though the club just avoided re-election after a number of heavy defeats, Henderson proved his opportunism in front of goal, scoring a hat-trick in a 7-3 defeat at Brentford. Towards the end of that 1932-33 campaign,he equalled the feats of Hughie Ferguson and Walter Robbins when he netted five of the club's goals in a 6-0 home win over Northampton Town to end the season with 12 goals in 16 League games.

In 1933-34 City finished bottom of the Third Division (South) and had to seek re-election though Henderson continued to find the net and was the club's second top scorer with 12 goals in 28 League games.

Henderson, who once scored six goals in a friendly match for the Ninian Park club was one of the players released by manager Watts-Jones prior to the 1934-35 season.

HEWITT, RON

Inside-forward Ron Hewitt was a junior with Wolverhampton Wanderers but after failing to make the grade at Molineux, he had a short spell with Walsall in 1949 before playing for Darlington. In 1951 he moved to

Wrexham and in his first season with the Robins, topped the club's scoring charts with 16 goals in 38 League games. After netting 13 in 1952-53 he headed the scoring lists again the following season with 15 goals. His best season in terms of goals scored was 1956-57 when he netted 22 goals in 31 games including hat-tricks against Barrow and Carlisle United. At the end of that season, Hewitt who had scored 111 goals in 267 League and Cup games joined Cardiff City for £7,000.

He made his debut in a goalless draw at home to rivals Swansea Town on the opening day of the 1957-58 season, a campaign in which he was the club's leading scorer with 14 League goals. His total included his first hat-trick for the club in a 4-3 home win over Blackburn Rovers.

Within months of his arrival at Ninian Park, Hewitt won his first full Welsh cap when he played against Northern Ireland and went on to make four more appearances for his country including three in the 1958 World Cup Finals in Sweden.

He topped the Bluebirds' scoring charts again in 1958-59 before leaving Ninian Park and returning to Wrexham.

After just one season at the Racecourse Ground, he joined Coventry City for £4,500. He later ended his League career with Chester before playing non-League football for Hereford United, Northwich Victoria, Witton Albion and Caernarfon.

HITCHENS, GERRY

Gerry Hitchens signed for Kidderminster Harriers in 1953 and after turning in some outstanding performances was signed by Cardiff City in January 1955 for £1,500. Within three months he had made his first team debut for the Bluebirds, scoring in a 3-2 home win over Wolverhampton Wanderers in a match City had to win to avoid relegation.

Forming a formidable partnership with Trevor Ford, he was the club's leading scorer for the next two seasons and in 1956-57 became the first City player to score over 20 League goals since Stan Richards' 30 goals in 1946-47.

In 1955-56 when Cardiff won the Welsh Cup, Hitchens scored 12 goals in the four games leading up to the final including five goals in a 7-0 win at Oswestry and hat-tricks in the 9-0 win over Pembroke Borough and the 5-3 defeat of Wrexham.

He had scored 40 goals in 95 League appearances for the Ninian Park club when in December 1957 he was sold to Aston Villa for £22,500.

Hitchens was an explosive striker who had a flair for scoring goals and gave early notice of his talents by scoring three goals in his first three games for the Villa Park club.

His first hat-trick for Villa came the following season when he scored all the goals in a 3-1 win over Bolton Wanderers. During the 1959-60 season, Hitchens scored ten goals in three successive games, including five in the 11-1 defeat of Charlton Athletic which equalled the club record for the most goals scored by one player in a League game.

That season he topped the club's goalscoring charts with 23 League goals as they won the Second Division championship. In 1960-61 he achieved the feat again, this time with 29 goals. He also helped Villa to the League Cup final, scoring in every round of the competition.

Despite those 11 goals, he missed the final against Rotherham United because by the time it was played, he had joined Italian giants Inter Milan. The England international, who scored with his first touch on his debut against Mexico, stayed in Italy for eight years, playing for Torino, Atalanta and Cagliari. He returned to England in 1969 to play for Worcester City and retired after a short spell with Merthyr Tydfil. Gerry Hitchens died aged only 48, whilst playing in a charity match in North Wales in 1983.

HOLE, BARRIE

The son of a pre-war Welsh international, Barrie Hole, a Swansea Town player, did not follow in his father's footsteps like his two older brothers who both joined the Vetch Field club, preferring to join Cardiff City.

He made his first team debut at the age of 17 years 170 days in a 4-3 win at Leyton Orient on 27 February 1960, in a season which saw the club win promotion to the First Division.

After getting another first team chance the following season, he established himself as a creative wing-half and inside-forward and rarely missed a game, being ever-present in 1964-65. Whilst at Ninian Park he won five Wales Under-23 caps and won the first of 30 full caps when he played against Northern Ireland in 1963.

He had played in 211 League games for the Bluebirds when in the summer of 1966 he left Ninian Park to join Blackburn Rovers for a fee of £40,000.

At Ewood Park he was the club's first specialist midfielder. An extraordinarily gifted ball player, he had the ability to ghost into the opposing penalty area completely unmarked, enabling him to score a number of important goals.

He had scored 15 goals in 88 League and Cup games for the Lancashire club when Aston Villa paid £60,000 for him in September 1968. He remained at Villa Park for two years when a £20,000 fee took him home to Wales and Swansea City.

HOLLYMAN, KEN

A versatile player, Ken Hollyman joined the club from Cardiff Nomads in 1941 and made 81 wartime appearances, scoring 13 goals before making his Football League debut in a 2-1 defeat at Norwich City in the opening game of the 1946-47 season.

Although on the small side, Hollyman was strong in the tackle and had an outstanding work-rate. He missed very few games in the immediate seasons following the hostilities and was the club's only ever-present in 1950-51 when the Bluebirds finished third in the Second Division.

He went on to play in 210 first team games for the Ninian Park club but after 12 years on the City staff, he left to join Newport County.

He was a great favourite at Somerton Park as he had been at Cardiff, playing in 231 League games before becoming player/coach at valleys club Ton Pentre.

HOME MATCHES

Cardiff City's best home wins are the 9-2 rout of Thames Association on 6 February 1932 in a Third Division (South) game and the 8-0 first round FA Cup win over Enfield in the same season. In the Welsh Cup, the Bluebirds defeated Knighton Town 16-0 in 1960-61 and Oswestry 10-0 in 1922-23.

City's worst home defeat is 9-1, a scoreline inflicted upon them by Wolverhampton Wanderers on 3 September 1955.

HOME SEASONS

Cardiff City have gone through a complete League season with an undefeated home record on just one occasion and that was in 1946-47 when they won 18 and drew three of their home matches in winning the Third Division (South) championship.

The club's highest number of home wins in a League season is 18 in the 1946-47 and 1951-52 seasons. The 1946-47 season saw the most number of goals scored at Ninian Park in a season, 63.

HONOURS

The major honours achieved by the club are:

Football League

Division 1 Runners-Up	1923-24		
Division 2 Runners-Up	1920-21	1951-52	1959-60
Division 3 (South) Champions	1946-47		
Division 3 Champions	1992-93		
Division 3 Runners-Up	1975-76	1982-83	
Division 4 Runners-Up	1987-88		
FA Cup Winners	1927		
FA Cup Runners-Up	1925		
FA Charity Shield Winners	1927		
Welsh Cup Winners	1912	1920	1922
	1923	1927	1928
	1930	1956	1959
	1964	1965	1967
	1968	1969	1970
	1971	1973	1974
	1976	1988	1992

Cardiff City 1946-47 Division III Champions

HOOPER, PETER

Though he only stayed for one season at Ninian Park, left-winger Peter Hooper was the club's top scorer with 24 League and Cup goals.

The Teignmouth-born player began his career with non-League Dawlish before joining Bristol Rovers in 1953. He soon established himself in the Rovers' first team and in nine seasons with the then Eastville club, proved himself a prolific marksman, scoring 102 goals in 295 League games.

He joined Cardiff City in the summer of 1962 and made his debut in a 4-4 draw at home to Newcastle United on the opening day of the 1962-63 season, scoring one of City's goals. After hitting five 'doubles' he netted a hat-trick in a 3-2 win at Luton Town, where his powerful left foot fired home goals from quite a distance.

At the end of that season, he had a disagreement with the City board over terms and left Ninian Park to join Bristol City for a fee of £11,250. The popular winger ended his League career with the Ashton Gate club where he took his total of League goals for his three clubs to 138 in 389 appearances.

HOWELLS, RON

Goalkeeper Ron Howells began his League career with his home-town club Swansea but had made only eight appearances for the Vetch Field club before being released and joined Barry Town. His performances for the Welsh League club led to Cardiff City signing the 'keeper in 1950. With Iorwerth Hughes the club's first choice goalkeeper, he had to wait until Boxing Day 1951 before making his first team debut. He gave a near faultless display in a 3-0 home win over his former club and after that, was a virtual ever-present for the next six seasons.

In that time, he played in 172 games for the club and won two full international caps for Wales in 1954 against England and Scotland.

After leaving Ninian Park, he played non-League football for Worcester City but in September 1958 he returned to League action with Chester City and went on to appear in 80 games for the Cestrians.

I

INJURIES

The risk of serious injury is an ever-present threat in the game of football and all professional players expect to miss games through injury at some point in their careers.

Welsh Under-23 international Steve Gammon broke his leg three times in the space of three seasons but was unable to recover full fitness after the last break and went into non-League football with Kettering Town in the Southern League.

When City entertained Aston Villa at Ninian Park on Boxing Day 1967 they were leading 1-0 at half-time. Full-back Graham Coldrick couldn't take the field for the second half with a knee injury and was substituted by Gary Bell.

In the 56th minute, City's Bobby Brown collided with Villa 'keeper Colin Withers and had to be stretchered off with a bad leg injury that ended his career. John Toshack had headed City into a 2-0 lead and despite going down to nine men when David Carver was carried off, the Bluebirds won the game 3-0 when the scorer of the first goal, Leslie Lea netted his second.

However, not every injury is sustained on the pitch of course. Jimmy Cringan's career was ended when he had an accident with a hand-grenade that damaged a leg, thus preventing him from playing League football again.

INTERNATIONAL MATCHES

Ninian Park replaced the Arms Park as Cardiff's football international venue, and following the first game against Scotland in March 1911, in which Wales drew 2-2, the ground has now staged 94 internationals.

The record gate for one of these international matches is also the ground's record gate, when 61,566 saw Wales draw 1-1 with England on 14 October 1961.

INTERNATIONAL PLAYERS

Cardiff City's most capped player (ie: caps gained while players were registered with the club) is Alf Sherwood with 39 caps for Wales. The following is a complete list of players who have gained full international honours while at Ninian Park.

Wales

I.J.Allchurch (12)	1963 v	Scotland, England, N.Ireland, Holland (2)
	1964 v	England
	1965 v	Scotland, England, N.Ireland, Greece, Italy, Russia
C.W.Baker (7)	1958 v	Mexico
	1960 v	Scotland, N.Ireland
	1961 v	Scotland, England, Eire
	1962 v	Scotland
W.G.Baker (1)	1948 v	N.Ireland
G.H.Beadles (2)	1925 v	England, Scotland
M.Charles (4)	1962 v	Brazil, N.Ireland
	1963 v	Scotland, Holland
J.Charles (3)	1964 v	Scotland
	1965 v	Scotland, Russia
A.Curtis (1)	1987 v	Russia
E.R.Curtis (1)	1928 v	Scotland
L.H.Davies (23)	1922 v	England, Scotland, N.Ireland
	1923 v	England, Scotland, N.Ireland
	1924 v	England, Scotland, N.Ireland
	1925 v	Scotland, N.Ireland
	1926 v	England, N.Ireland
	1927 v	England, N.Ireland
	1928 v	Scotland, N.Ireland, England
	1929 v	Scotland, N.Ireland, England

	1930 v	England, Scotland
W.Davies (8)	1925 v	England, Scotland, N.Ireland
	1926 v	England, Scotland, N.Ireland
	1927 v	Scotland
	1928 v	N.Ireland
S.C.Derrett (4)	1969 v	Scotland, W.Germany
	1970 v	Italy
	1971 v	Finland
P.Dwyer (10)	1978 v	Iran, England, Scotland, N.Ireland
	1979 v	Turkey, Scotland, England, N.Ireland, Malta
	1980 v	W.Germany
G.Edwards (6)	1949 v	N.Ireland, Portugal, Belgium, Switzerland
	1950 v	England, Scotland
H.P.Evans (6)	1922 v	England, Scotland, N.Ireland
	1924 v	England, Scotland, N.Ireland
J.Evans (8)	1912 v	N.Ireland
	1913 v	N.Ireland
	1914 v	Scotland
	1920 v	Scotland, N.Ireland
	1922 v	N.Ireland
	1923 v	England, N.Ireland
L.Evans (2)	1931 v	England, Scotland
T.Ford (10)	1954 v	Austria
	1955 v	Scotland, England, N.Ireland, Yugoslavia
	1956 v	Scotland, N.Ireland, England, Austria
	1957 v	Scotland
A.C.Harrington (11)	1956 v	N.Ireland
	1957 v	England, Scotland
	1958 v	Scotland, N.Ireland, Israel(2)
	1961 v	Scotland, England
	1962 v	England, Scotland
S.O.Haworth (1)	1997 v	Scotland
R.Hewitt (5)	1958 v	N.Ireland, Israel, Sweden, Holland, Brazil
B.G.Hole (18)	1963 v	N.Ireland
	1964 v	N.Ireland,
	1965 v	Scotland, England, N.Ireland, Denmark, Greece (2), Russia, Italy
	1966 v	England, Scotland, N.Ireland, Russia,

	Denmark, Brazil(2), Chile
R.G.Howells (2)	1954 v England, Scotland,
B.S.Jones (7)	1969 v Scotland, England, N.Ireland, Italy,
	W.Germany, E.Germany, Rest of UK
L.J.Jones (1)	1933 v France
F.C.Keenor (31)	1920 v England, N.Ireland
	1921 v England, N.Ireland, Scotland
	1922 v N.Ireland
	1923 v England, N.Ireland, Scotland
	1924 v England, N.Ireland, Scotland
	1925 v England, N.Ireland, Scotland
	1926 v Scotland
	1927 v England, N.Ireland, Scotland
	1928 v England, N.Ireland, Scotland
	1929 v England, N.Ireland, Scotland
	1930 v England, N.Ireland, Scotland
	1931 v England, N.Ireland, Scotland
G.Latham (1)	1913 v N.Ireland
J.Lewis (1)	1926 v Scotland
G.Moore (5)	1960 v England, Scotland, N.Ireland
	1961 v Eire, Spain
J.Nicholls (2)	1925 v England, Scotland
J.Perry (1)	1994 v Norway
L.Phillips (12)	1971 v Czechoslovakia, Scotland, England,
	N.Ireland
	1972 v Czechoslovakia, Romania, Scotland,
	N.Ireland
	1973 v England
	1974 v Poland, N.Ireland
	1975 v Austria
K.Pontin (2)	1980 v England, Scotland
G.I.Reece (13)	1973 v England, N.Ireland
	1974 v Poland, England, Scotland, N.Ireland
	1975 v Austria, Holland (2) Luxembourg (2),
	Scotland, N.Ireland
W.Rees (3)	1949 v N.Ireland, Belgium, Switzerland
S.V.Richards (1)	1947 v England
W.W.Robbins (5)	1931 v England, Scotland
	1932 v England, N.Ireland, Scotland

P.J.Rodrigues (7)	1965 v	N.Ireland, Greece (2)
	1966 v	Russia, England, Scotland, Denmark
P.Sayer (7)	1977 v	Czechoslovakia, Scotland, England, N.Ireland
	1978 v	Kuwait (2), Scotland
A.T.Sherwood (39)	1947 v	England, N.Ireland
	1948 v	Scotland, N.Ireland
	1949 v	England, Scotland, N.Ireland, Portugal, Switzerland
	1950 v	England, Scotland, N.Ireland, Belgium,
	1951 v	England, Scotland, N.Ireland, Portugal, Switzerland
	1952 v	England, Scotland, N.Ireland, Rest of UK
	1953 v	Scotland, England, N.Ireland, France, Yugoslavia
	1954 v	England, Scotland, N.Ireland, Austria
	1955 v	Scotland, England, Yugoslavia, N.Ireland
	1956 v	England, Scotland, N.Ireland, Austria
D.Showers (2)	1975 v	England, N.Ireland
F.Stansfield (1)	1949 v	Scotland
R.F.Stitfall (2)	1953 v	England
	1957 v	Czechoslovakia
D.Sullivan (17)	1953 v	N.Ireland, France, Yugoslavia
	1954 v	N.Ireland
	1955 v	England N.Ireland
	1957 v	England, Scotland
	1958 v	Sweden, Brazil, N.Ireland, Holland (2)
	1959 v	Scotland, N.Ireland
	1960 v	England, Scotland
D.R.Tapscott (2)	1959 v	England, N.Ireland
R.J.Thomas (1)	1978 v	Czechoslovakia
J.B.Toshack (8)	1969 v	Scotland, England, N.Ireland, W.Germany, E.Germany, Rest of UK
	1970 v	E.Germany, Italy
N.Vaughan (7)	1984 v	Romania, Bulgaria, Yugoslavia, N.Ireland, Norway, Israel
	1985 v	Spain
G.Vearncombe (2)	1958 v	E.Germany
	1961 v	Eire

A.K.Villars (3)   1974 v England, Scotland, N.Ireland
D.Ward (1)   1962 v England
F.W.Warren (1)   1929 v N.Ireland
G.J.J.Williams (1)   1951 v Switzerland

Scotland
J.Blair (6)   1921 v England
                     1922 v England
                     1923 v England, Wales, N.Ireland
                     1924 v Wales
J.Nelson (4)   1925 v Wales, N.Ireland
                     1928 v England
                     1930 v France

Northern Ireland
T.G.Farquharson (7) 1923 v Scotland, Wales
                     1924 v England, Scotland, Wales
                     1925 v England, Scotland
S.J.Irving (6)   1927 v Scotland, England, Wales
                     1928 v Scotland, England, Wales
J.McCambridge (2)   1931 v Wales
                     1932 v England
G.H.Reid (1)   1923 v Scotland
T.Sloan (8)   1926 v Scotland, Wales, England
                     1927 v Wales, Scotland
                     1928 v England, Wales
                     1929 v England
E.E.Smith (4)   1921 v Scotland
                     1923 v Wales, England
                     1924 v England
T.Watson (1)   1926 v Scotland

Republic of Ireland
T.G.Farquharson (4) 1929 v Belgium
                     1930 v Belgium
                     1931 v Spain
                     1932 v Spain
R.Healey (2)   1977 v Poland
                     1980 v England

IRWIN, BILL

Irish amateur international goalkeeper Bill Irwin began his career with Irish League club Bangor before joining Cardiff City in October 1971.

During his early days with the Bluebirds, he made a number of outstanding saves, perhaps none more so than in City's 2-0 fifth round FA Cup defeat at home to Leeds United in February 1972 when it won him the BBC TV's 'Save of the Season' award.

After making his debut in a 2-1 home defeat by Millwall, Irwin went on to be the club's first choice 'keeper for four seasons beating off Parsons, Eadie and Grotier until the arrival of Ron Healey in 1974.

During the Welsh Cup Final of 1973, Irwin had the unenviable distinction of being the first Cardiff City goalkeeper to be sent off when he received his marching orders against Bangor City.

He went on to appear in 222 first team games for the Bluebirds before leaving in 1977 to join Vancouver Whitecaps.

J

JAMES, BILLY

After signing professional forms for Cardiff City in October 1938, the 17-year-old Billy James looked destined to have a great future. His career was interrupted by the Second World War and he had to wait until 1946 before making his Football League debut.

During the early part of the hostilities, James played for Wales in international matches and in games for Cardiff, scored 41 goals in 56 games including 29 goals in 29 appearances during the 1940-41 season. One of the most talented inside-forwards ever to play for the club, he scored three hat-tricks in that campaign - Swansea Town (Home 8-0), Stoke City (Home 4-0) and Bath City (Home 5-2).

After joining the Army, James was taken prisoner by the Japanese and spent four years in a Prisoner of War camp. Sadly his sight had been affected and when League football resumed in 1946, he only played in six games, scoring two goals, before he became Coach at the club.

JENNINGS, BILLY

Born in Barry, Billy Jennings played his early football with Bethel Baptists in his home town. He was capped by Wales Schoolboys in 1907 when he played against England at Walsall and he was then signed by Bolton in August 1912. In February 1914, he was still in the Wanderers' Reserve side even though he won the first of 11 full caps against Scotland in Glasgow. After serving in the Royal Flying Corps during the First World War he won a regular place in the Bolton side and in 1923 played in all seven FA Cup ties when the club won the trophy. He was also in the team again in 1926 when the Wanderers beat Manchester City 1-0. He retired from playing in 1931 to become coach at Notts County after appearing in 287 League and Cup games for the Trotters.

In 1936 he was appointed Cardiff City's chief coach but a year later replaced Watts-Jones as the club's secretary-manager. At Ninian Park, Jennings faced the job of rebuilding a team despite having little money due to a fire at the ground that destroyed the stands and offices. He bought a number of players from his former club and signed former England fullback Ernie Blenkinsop as coach in November 1938. Five months later he was replaced by Cyril Spiers.

JOHN, DILWYN

Goalkeeper Dilwyn John was just 17 years 109 days old when he made his first team debut for the Bluebirds in a 3-2 win at Chelsea on 20 September 1961. He went on to appear in 21 League games that season sharing the 'keepers duties with Swan and Vearncombe. Unfortunately, at the end of the campaign, City lost their First Division status. Over the next six seasons, John played in 99 first team games and won a Welsh Under-23 cap but his slender physique meant that he never developed into one of the club's greatest goalkeepers.

In 1967 he left Ninian Park and joined Swansea Town, appearing in 80 League games for the Swans in three years at the Vetch Field. After leaving Swansea, he played non-League football for Hereford United and Merthyr Tydfil.

JONES, BARRIE

Swansea-born Barrie Jones began his career with his home-town team as a winger in the traditional mould. In five years at the Vetch Field he was capped eight times at Welsh Under-23 level and won the first of 15 full caps when he played against Scotland in 1963.

After scoring 23 goals in 166 appearances for the Swans he joined Plymouth Argyle in 1964 for a fee of £45,000, then the Home Park club's highest-ever payment for a player. It was Jones' exceptional ball-control which Argyle manager Malcolm Allison was seeking to incorporate into his team plans. In three seasons at Home Park he scored nine goals in 99 games but in March 1967, the fair-haired little winger signed for the Bluebirds for £25,000.

He played his first game for the club in a 2-0 defeat at Northampton Town but then shortly switched from the wing into midfield. His play improved so much that he went on to win seven international caps with Cardiff compared to just one during his stay with Plymouth. Jones was ever-present in season's 1967-68 and 1968-69, playing in 107 consecutive League games from his debut. On 4 October 1969 he broke his leg in the last minute of City's 3-2 defeat at Blackpool, and though he attempted a number of comebacks in the Reserves he never regained full fitness and had to hang up his boots at League level.

Though never a prolific scorer with the Ninian Park club, netting 18 goals in 107 appearances, he did once score a hat-trick in the club's 5-0 win over Mauritius in May 1969.

Jones had a number of seasons playing non-League football before going into business in the Swansea area.

JONES, BILL

Bill Jones made only 23 Football League appearances in eight seasons with Newport County before moving into non-League football with Barry Town. When his playing days were over he became chief scout for Ipswich Town before being appointed manager of Barry Town in 1950. It was here that he discovered Derek Tapscott and Dai Ward.

Jones arrived at Ninian Park in 1957 as assistant-manager and chief scout to Trevor Morris, whom he succeeded a year later. He took the Bluebirds into the First Division in 1960 and helped to produce talented players such as Alan Durban, Barrie Hole and Graham Moore. City were relegated at the end of the 1961-62 season and after a bad start to the following campaign, Jones was dismissed and rejoined Worcester City whom he had managed prior to coming to Cardiff.

JONES, LESLIE

Inside-forward Leslie Jones began his career with his home-town club Aberdare Athletic before joining Cardiff City in 1929. After making his debut in a 1-0 defeat at Vetch Field in February 1930 he struck up a formidable left-wing partnership with Walter Robbins. Over the next five seasons he played in 161 League and Cup games with his most prolific season being 1932-33 when he scored 16 goals. His performances during that campaign led to him winning the first of 11 Welsh caps when he played against France.

His all-action displays in the Christmas matches of 1933 persuaded

Coventry City manager Harry Storer to pay £2,000 for him. In nearly five years at Highfield Road, he scored at a rate of a goal in every other game (74 in 144). In 1935-36 he won a Third Division (South) championship medal and though Coventry resisted a £7,000 bid from Tottenham Hotspur, they could not refuse Arsenal's offer in 1937.

He helped the Gunners win the League Championship in 1937-38 and in the last season before the Second World war, he won an FA Charity Shield winners' medal against Preston North End.

During the hostilities he continued to play for the Highbury club and won five wartime caps. On the return of peace, he was granted a free transfer and moved to Swansea Town as player-coach. His stay at the Vetch Field was short lived and he became player-manager of Barry Town, before returning to League football with Brighton, where in 1948-49, he finished his long career. He later managed Scunthorpe United.

JONES, LINDEN

Full-back Linden Jones worked his way up through the club's ranks to make his first team debut in a 1-0 home win over Leyton Orient on 24 February 1979. Four days later he achieved the unenviable record of being the youngest player in the history of Cardiff City to be sent off when he received his marching orders in the club's 4-1 win at Blackburn Rovers.

He missed very few games over the next five seasons and in 1982-83 he was outstanding as the club won promotion.

Jones went on to play in 165 first team games during his Ninian Park career before joining Newport County in September 1983.

He played in 141 League games for the Somerton Park club but when it faced closure in 1987 he joined Reading where he appeared in 152 League games before a series of injuries ended his career.

JOSLIN, PHIL

Goalkeeper Phil Joslin began his Football League career with Torquay United and before the outbreak of the Second World War, appeared in 135 League games for the Devon club. During the hostilities he was stationed in London and 'guested' for a number of clubs including Arsenal, Fulham and Tottenham Hotspur.

When League football resumed in 1946, Joslin continued to play for the Plainmoor club until joining the Bluebirds in the summer of 1948 and made his debut in a 3-0 defeat at Bradford Park Avenue in the opening game of the 1948-49 season. In that campaign he kept 15 clean sheets in

38 appearances including four in successive games on two occasions. A virtual ever-present for three seasons at Ninian Park, he had played in 124 first team games for City when he broke his leg in a goalmouth collision with Wilf Grant during a public trial match prior to the 1951-52 season.

The injury brought an end to the popular 'keeper's career.

JUBILEE FUND

The League Benevolent Fund was launched in 1938, fifty years after the start of the Football League, to benefit players who had fallen on hard times.

It was decided that the best way to raise funds was for sides to play local 'derby' games with no account being taken of League status. City played Swansea Town at the Vetch Field before that start of the 1938-39 season and shared six goals, with the Ninian Park club's goals being scored by Jimmy Collins (2) and a Simmons own goal. The return game played at Ninian Park just before the start of the ill-fated 1939-40 season, also ended all-square at 1-1 with Ernie Marshall netting for the Bluebirds.

K

KEATING, ALBERT

Albert Keating joined Newcastle United from Prudhoe Castle but in two years at St James' Park, he only made 12 appearances. In November 1925 he joined Bristol City and the following season helped them win promotion from the Third Division. He was the Ashton Gate club's leading scorer in 1927-28 but after scoring 49 goals in 81 games, he returned north to play for Blackburn Rovers. The Ewood Park club were in the First Division and Keating struggled to win a regular place, making just 17 appearances in three seasons with the Lancashire club.

He arrived at Ninian Park towards the end of the 1930-31 season and made his debut in a 4-0 defeat at Barnsley. Though he failed to score in six appearances that season, he scored 23 goals in 38 League and Cup games in 1931-32 including a hat-trick in the 8-0 FA Cup win over Enfield.

After a brief spell with Bristol City, Keating returned to the north-east to play non-League football.

KEATING, REG

Reg Keating had an unusual career as he alternated between the Football League and non-League. The brother of Albert Keating, he began his career with Newcastle United but without playing a game for them, he joined Gainsborough Trinity and then Scarborough Town before playing for Stockport County. He made his Football League debut for the Edgeley Park club in a 3-2 win over Hull City on the opening day of the 1930-31 season. After just five appearances for County he played for Birmingham where he scored 36 goals in Central League games and then Norwich City before joining Cardiff.

He played his first match for the Bluebirds in March 1934 as they beat Queen's Park Rangers 3-1 and the following month netted his first hat-trick for the club in a 3-1 win at Aldershot.

The following season he was the club's leading scorer with 20 League goals, helping City to avoid finishing bottom of the Third Division (South). In the penultimate match of the season he netted four goals in a 5-0 home win over Exeter City. He was the club's top scorer again in 1935-36 with 10 League goals including his third hat-trick for the Bluebirds in a 4-2 win at Millwall.

He later played for Doncaster Rovers and Bournemouth before ending his career with Carlisle United.

KEENOR, FRED

After having been capped at outside-right in 1907 in the first schoolboy international between England and Wales, he joined Cardiff City as an amateur inside-forward four years later. He turned professional in 1912 and made his Southern League debut in a 1-1 home draw against Exeter City in December of 1913. At the outbreak of the First World War, he joined the 'Footballers Battalion' (17th Middlesex) and was twice wounded in action. At the end of the hostilities he returned to Cardiff and made his first appearance for Wales in the Victory internationals.

When City entered the Football League, he scored in the club's first League game in a 5-2 win at Stockport County. Succeeding Charlie Brittan as captain, he led both his club and country to success. He led Wales to the Home International Championship in 1924, and was part of the 1925 Bluebirds team that lost to Sheffield United in the FA Cup Final. He returned to Wembley two years later as victorious captain in the 1-0 defeat of Arsenal.

Keenor who made 32 appearances for his country, was an inspirational captain. His will to win, coupled with his uncompromising tackling made him a tough opponent. He went on to appear in 436 League and Cup games for a club he had done much to establish before leaving to join Crewe Alexandra after 19 years at Ninian Park.

In three years at Gresty Road he made 116 League appearances before going into non-League football, first with Oswestry and then as player-manager of Tunbridge Wells. A serious illness ended the career of a man who had become a legend in Welsh football.

KING, PETER

Peter King played his early football for his home-town team, Worcester City before joining Cardiff City in 1960. One of the most versatile players in the club's history, he made his City debut in a 2-1 defeat at Burnley in October 1961 in a First Division match.

He kept his place for most of the remainder of that season but then missed the majority of the 1962-63 campaign with a chest illness. The following season he had fully recovered and scored both Cardiff's goals in a 2-0 Welsh Cup Final replay win over Bangor City.

In 1964-65 King scored his only Football League hat-trick for the club in a 6-1 home win over Middlesbrough and netted the Bluebirds' first goal in Europe when he scored the only goal of the two-legged tie against Esjberg.

He missed very few games over the next few seasons and in 1967-68 was ever-present and the club's top scorer with 12 League goals and six more in Cup competitions.

In 1970-71 he missed just one game as City finished third in Division Two but an achilles tendon injury forced him to quit the game in 1974 after this most loyal of Cardiff City clubmen had scored 108 goals in 469 first team games in 13 seasons at Ninian Park.

Peter King in action for Cardiff City against QPR.
Cardiff City 4 QPR 2 - September 27th 1969 (Att: 30,083)

KITCHEN, PETER

After scoring 89 goals in 228 League games for Doncaster Rovers he became one of the prized assets of the lower divisions and it came as no surprise when Orient paid £40,000 to take him to Brisbane Road in the summer of 1977. He continued to score goals for Orient and in two years with the club netted 28 in 65 League games including the only goal of the final game of the 1977-78 season to save the London club from relegation.

He moved across the capital to play for Fulham but he failed to settle at Craven Cottage and in the summer of 1980 he joined Cardiff City for £100,000.

He made his debut for the Bluebirds against one of his former clubs, Orient on 30 August 1982 but failed to score in a 4-2 win for the Welsh club. He ended the season as top scorer with 13 League goals and netted five in the 6-0 Welsh Cup win over Cardiff Corinthians. He lost form midway through the following season and having scored 30 goals in 74 games left to play for Orient again after a spell in Hong Kong, before ending his career at Chester.

KNEESHAW, JACK

Goalkeeper Jack Kneeshaw was a loyal servant of Cardiff City Football Club both as a player and after his career had ended. After failing to make much impression with his home-town club Bradford City, he tried his luck with both Guiseley and Colne and it was from the latter club that City manager Fred Stewart signed him in the summer of 1912.

After making his Southern League debut in a 1-1 draw at Swansea on the opening day of the 1912-13 season, Kneeshaw went on to be a virtual ever-present, playing in 111 games in four seasons.

He was still the club's first-choice goalkeeper when the Bluebirds entered the Football League for the 1920-21 season and played in the club's first-ever match, a 5-2 win at Stockport County. He went on to appear in 34 League games, eventually losing his place to Ben Davies.

After his playing days were over, he became a member of the club's training staff and in the late 1930s, he was appointed as City's coach. Despite being replaced by Ernie Blenkinsop, he stayed at Ninian Park working behind the scenes.

L

LARGEST CROWD

It was on 14 October 1961 that Ninian Park housed its largest crowd. The occasion was the Wales v England international, when a staggering crowd of 61,566 saw the teams play out a 1-1 draw.

The largest crowd for a game involving Cardiff City is 57,893 for the First Division encounter against Arsenal on 22 April 1953. For the record, the game was goalless.

LARMOUR, ALBERT

Belfast-born defender Albert Larmour joined City from Irish League club Linfield for a fee of £12,000 in the summer of 1972.

However, after making his debut in a 2-1 home win over Luton Town on the opening day of the 1972-73 season, he failed to win a regular place in the Cardiff line-up and over the next two seasons made just seven League appearances.

It was 1974-75 when Larmour established himself as a first team regular, a season when he scored his only goal for the club. It came in the second leg of the Welsh Cup Final, which City lost 5-2 on aggregate to Wrexham. In 1975-76 he played an important role as sweeper as the club won promotion to the Second Division. He went on to appear in 201 first team games for City, losing his place midway through the 1978-79 season when the Bluebirds paid £65,000 to sign Dave Roberts from Hull City.

He then joined Torquay United and after immediately being made club captain, went on to score four goals in 50 League games before leaving the Plainmoor club.

LATE FINISHES

Cardiff's final match of the season against Leyton Orient at Ninian Park on 7 June 1947 is the latest date for the finish of any Bluebirds' season. The season which had been extended into June because of the severe winter saw City win the Third Division (South) championship. For the record, Leyton Orient were beaten 1-0 with Billy Rees scoring the City goal.

LATE GOALS

On 29 January 1977 at Ninian Park, Cardiff City were leading Wrexham 2-1 in the FA Cup fourth round when Graham Whittle equalised for the Robins in the dying seconds of the game. There was just time for City to restart and score themselves through John Buchanan before the final whistle went at 3-2 for the Bluebirds.

LATHAM, GEORGE

George Latham was one of the most influential men in Welsh football. Born in Newtown mid Wales in 1880, he was a noted footballer in his youth who could play in a variety of positions. After fighting in the Boer War he returned to join Liverpool and it was whilst playing for the Anfield club that he won the first of his ten Welsh caps, playing at right-half against Scotland in a 3-1 win at Wrexham in 1905. After a spell with Southport Central and Stoke, he joined Cardiff City and in 1912 he helped them beat Pontypridd 3-0 to win the Welsh Cup.

His last game for Wales came in 1913 under very strange circumstances. He had retired from the international scene and was accompanying the Welsh team to Ireland as trainer. During the journey, two of the Welsh side were taken ill and Latham was asked to deputise. He gave a solid performance in a 1-0 win for Wales.

During the First World War whilst on operations in Gaza he was twice decorated for bravery as a Captain and was awarded the Military Cross. After the hostilities had ended he returned to Ninian Park as the club's trainer but was pressed into first team action at Blackburn Rovers on 2 January 1922 at the age of 41 when both Jack Evans and Jimmy Gill had been taken ill. Even then the City side was too strong for the Ewood Park side, winning 3-1.

Not surprisingly it was Latham's only Football League appearance for the Bluebirds.

He trained the club's 1925 and 1927 FA Cup Final teams and remained Welsh team trainer through the 1920s and early 1930s.

In 1932 he joined Chester, helping them to win the Welsh Cup but two years later he returned to Cardiff. He died aged 58 just before the outbreak of the Second World War.

LEADING SCORERS
Cardiff City have provided the Football League's divisional leading goalscorer on just one occasion. That was in 1968-69 when John Toshack topped the Second Division goalscoring charts with 22 goals.

LEAGUE GOALS - CAREER HIGHEST
Len Davies holds the Ninian Park record for the most League goals with a career total of 129 between 1920 and 1931.

LEAGUE GOALS - LEAST CONCEDED
During the 1946-47 season, City conceded just 30 goals when winning the Third Division (South) championship.

LEAGUE GOALS - MOST CONCEDED
Cardiff City conceded 105 League goals in 1933-34 when they finished bottom of the Third Division (South).

LEAGUE GOALS - MOST INDIVIDUAL
Stan Richards holds the Cardiff City record for the most League goals in a season with 30 scored in the Third Division (South) championship-winning season of 1946-47.

LEAGUE GOALS - MOST SCORED
Cardiff City's highest goals tally in the Football League was during the 1946-47 Third Division (South) championship-winning season when they scored 93 goals.

LEEDS UNITED
Cardiff City drew Leeds United in the third round of the FA Cup in three successive years between 1955 and 1958, winning 2-1 on each occasion.

LEVER, ARTHUR
Better known as 'Buller', Arthur Lever joined Cardiff City in 1943 and

made 104 wartime appearances for the club before making his League debut in a 2-1 defeat at Norwich City on the opening day of the 1946-47. He went on to become the club's only ever-present that season as the Bluebirds won the Third Division (South) championship.

He was ever-present again the following season when he scored in both matches against the Second Division runners-up Newcastle United, from his position at right-back. He went on to make 114 consecutive League appearances from his debut until he was injured in City's 1-0 win at Tottenham Hotspur in March 1949.

The popular full-back made 168 first team appearances for the Bluebirds before joining Leicester City in September 1950 for a fee of £17,000. In three seasons with the Filbert Street club, he made 113 League appearances and in 1953 won a Welsh international cap when he played against Scotland. He left Leicester in the summer of 1954 to join Fred Stansfield at Newport County where he saw out his League career.

LEWIS, JOHN

Born in Tredegar, John Lewis was spotted playing for Pontllanfraith in a Welsh League match and when offered terms, jumped at the chance. He made his debut for the Bluebirds in a 2-0 home win over Blackburn Rovers in September 1978 and for the next five seasons was a permanent fixture in the Cardiff side.

In 1982-83 when the club won promotion to the Second Division, he played in 39 League games, scoring five goals. He was a lucky omen because whenever Lewis scored in that season, the Bluebirds won, one of his strikes coming in the 2-0 win over Orient, the game in which the club clinched promotion.

Lewis had scored 11 goals in 163 first team games when in 1983 he moved to Newport County. He appeared in 153 League games for the Somerton Park side, scoring eight goals and though he was made player-manager when Jimmy Mullen left County, he couldn't prevent them being relegated to the Fourth Division in 1986-87. After Newport he joined Swansea City and made 25 League appearances.

LEYLAND DAF CUP

The Leyland Daf Cup replaced the Sherpa Van Trophy for the 1989-90 season. In an extraordinary first match, City lost 5-3 at home to Walsall and then went down 4-0 at Shrewsbury with a side that contained a number of reserve players.

In 1990-91 City lost 1-0 at home to Exeter City before a goal from Cohen Griffith gave them a 1-1 draw at Hereford United. Unfortunately, it wasn't enough to take the Bluebirds through to the knockout stages.

LIVERMORE, DOUG

Doug Livermore began his career with Liverpool where he was given the chance to replace Ian St John, as Bill Shankly set about reshaping his ageing team. He enjoyed a 13-match run towards the end of the 1969-70 season but in November 1970 he joined Norwich City for £22,000.

At Carrow Road he helped the Canaries gain promotion to the First Division in his first full campaign in East Anglia. He appeared in 131 League and Cup games for Norwich and had a loan spell at Bournemouth before joining Cardiff City in the summer of 1975.

He made his debut in a 1-1 home draw against Bury in the second match of the 1975-76 season and didn't miss a match as the club won promotion to the Second Division. Also that season he played in all of the club's eight Welsh Cup ties including the win over Hereford United in the final. Livermore played in 115 first team games for City before moving to Chester where he ended his League career.

He returned to Ninian Park in 1978 as first team coach before moving to Vetch Field as John Toshack's assistant. He later worked with the Welsh national team before becoming assistant-manager of Tottenham Hotspur.

LONG SERVICE

Cardiff City have had a number of players, managers and administrators who have given the club years of loyal service.

The founder of the club, Bartley Wilson who had seen it grow from the Riverside Cricket Club was secretary for 34 years before he replaced Fred Stewart as manager in 1933. It wasn't a happy time for him as the club stayed firmly rooted to the foot of the Third Division (South) and he was relieved to return to work in a backroom capacity with the club.

Fred Stewart who became the club's first secretary-manager in 1911, was in office for 22 years until his retirement in 1933. He brought George Latham to the club in March 1911 and he trained both the 1925 and 1927 FA Cup Final teams. He stayed with the club until 1932 before joining Chester, though he returned for two years later in the decade until ill-health forced his retirement. Stewart's greatest signing was Billy Hardy who played in 353 League games between 1911 and 1932.

Other players who have given the club long service are Jack Evans

(1910-1926); Fred Keenor (1912-1931); Tom Farquharson (1922-1935); Alf Sherwood (1941-1956); Ron Stitfall (1942-1964); Derek Sullivan (1947-1960); Peter King (1960-1974); Don Murray (1962-1974); and Phil Dwyer (1971-1985).

LOWEST

The lowest number of goals scored by Cardiff City in a single Football League season is 36 in 1974-75. The club's lowest points record in the Football League occurred in 1933-34 when the Bluebirds gained just 24 points and finished bottom of the Third Division (South).

M

MALLOY, DANNY

Signed from Dundee for £17,500, centre-half Danny Malloy had already been capped by Scotland at 'B' international level when he joined Cardiff City in 1955.

He made his debut in a 3-1 home win over Charlton Athletic, a match in which Neil O'Halloran also making his debut, scored a hat-trick.

An ever-present in 1956-57 when he scored his only League goal for the club from the penalty-spot in a 3-1 defeat at Manchester United, he went on to appear in 69 consecutive League games from his debut. Malloy was also ever-present in 1958-59 and 1960-61 and missed just one game in 1959-60.

In that 1959-60 season, Malloy was captain and led the club back to the top flight as runners-up to Aston Villa. That campaign also saw the Scottish defender score two own goals in the opening match when City beat Liverpool 3-2.

In 1960-61, Malloy did score another goal in Cardiff colours as Knighton Town were beaten 16-0 in a Welsh Cup tie.

In the summer of 1961, Malloy who had appeared in 262 first team games failed to agree terms for the coming season and left to become player-coach of Doncaster Rovers.

MANAGERS

This is a complete list of Cardiff City's full-time managers with the inclusive dates in which they held office:

Davy McDougall	1910-1911	Jimmy Andrews	1974-1978
Fred Stewart	1911-1933	Richie Morgan	1978-1982
Bartley Wilson	1933-1934	Len Ashurst	1982-1984
Ben Watts-Jones	1934-1937	Jimmy Goodfellow	1984
Billy Jennings	1937-1939	Alan Durban	1984-1986
Cyril Spiers	1939-1946	Frank Burrows	1986-1989
Billy McCandless	1946-1948	Len Ashurst	1989-1991
Cyril Spiers	1948-1954	Eddie May	1991-1994
Trevor Morris	1954-1958	Terry Yorath	1994-1995
Bill Jones	1958-1962	Eddie May	1995
George Swindin	1962-1964	Phil Neal	1996
Jimmy Scoular	1964-1973	Russell Osman	1996-1998
Frank O'Farrell	1973-1974	Frank Burrows	1998-

MARATHON MATCHES

Cardiff City have been involved in a number of cup games that have gone to three matches. These are Watford (FA Cup 1922-23); Darlington (FA Cup 1924-25); Manchester City (FA Cup 1960-61); Wrexham (League Cup 1963-64); York City (FA Cup 1969-70); Sunderland (FA Cup 1971-72); Bolton Wanderers (FA Cup 1972-73); and Millwall (FA Cup 1986-87).

MARKSMEN - LEAGUE

Cardiff City's top League goalscorer is Len Davies who struck 128 League goals during his twelve years at Ninian Park. He is the only player to have scored more than 100 League goals for the club.

1	Len Davies	128
2	Jimmy Gill	82
3	Brian Clark	79
4	Hughie Ferguson	76
5	John Toshack	74
6 =	Carl Dale	71
	Derek Tapscott	71
8 =	Peter King	67
	Chris Pike	67
10	Wilf Grant	65

MARKSMEN - OVERALL

Six players have hit a century of goals for the Bluebirds. The club's top marksman is Len Davies. The Century Club consists of:

1	Len Davies	184
2 =	Brian Clark	108
	Peter King	108
4 =	Carl Dale	103
	Jimmy Gill	103
6	John Toshack	100

MAY, EDDIE

Eddie May began his career as a centre-forward with Athenian League club Dagenham before a switch to full-back alerted Southend United. He went on to play in 111 League games for the Roots Hall club before joining Wrexham for £5,000 in the summer of 1968.

Over the next eight seasons he missed very few games being ever-present in season's 1971-72 and 1975-76.

Captain for much of his time at the Racecourse Ground, he led the Robins to the sixth round of the FA Cup in 1973-74 and to the quarter-finals of the European Cup Winners' Cup in 1975-76. At the end of that season May, who had played in 410 first team games, scoring 44 goals, joined Swansea City on a free transfer.

He made 90 League appearances for the Vetch Field club before taking up coaching posts with Leicester City and Charlton Athletic. After managing Newport County who had just lost their League status, he took charge at Cardiff City in July 1991.

In his first season at Ninian Park, the Bluebirds just missed the play-offs but in 1992-93, the club won the Third Division title with 83 points. Also that season, City won the Welsh Cup beating Rhyl 5-0 in the final at Cardiff Arms Park to gain entry into the European Cup Winners' Cup. The only hiccup that season was the first round FA Cup defeat against non-League Bath City. After finishing 19th in the Second Division in 1993-94, City lost to non-League Enfield in the following season's FA Cup competition and in November 1994, May was sacked. Four months later following the departure of Terry Yorath, May returned to take charge of the Bluebirds for a second time. Later that year, he left Ninian Park to manage Torquay United.

McCAMBRIDGE, JIM

Irish-born forward Jim McCambridge played his early football with Larne and Ballymena before moving to play in the Football League with Everton. At Goodison Park, McCambridge spent most of his time as understudy to Dixie Dean and only played in one League game when Everton won 3-0 at Bradford City.

He joined Cardiff City in January 1931 and scored both the club's goals in a 3-2 defeat at West Bromwich Albion. He ended that season with nine goals in 18 League games including netting a hat-trick in a 3-2 home win over Stoke City.

McCambridge won the third of his four full international caps for Ireland in 1931 when he played against Wales.

In 1931-32, he established a new club League goalscoring record when he hit 26 League goals including hat-tricks against Queen's Park Rangers (Away 3-2) and Clapton Orient (Home 5-0). He was the club's leading scorer again the following season with 16 goals after netting 11 in the first 12 games of the campaign.

Surprisingly, McCambridge who had scored 55 goals in 109 games for Cardiff was allowed to join Bristol Rovers in 1933. He headed their scoring charts in his first season at Eastville and had scored 23 goals in 57 games when he left to sign for Exeter City. The prolific marksman again topped the scoring charts with 16 goals in just 23 games before moving to play First Division football with Sheffield Wednesday. His stay at Hillsborough was brief and after just two appearances he joined Hartlepool United where he ended his League career.

McCANDLESS, BILLY

One of the great characters of the game, Billy McCandless has the unique record of having taken three separate South Wales sides to the Third Division (South) championship.

He played in three Irish Cup finals for Linfield before moving to Ibrox Park where he gained seven League Championship medals in Rangers' great side of that time. McCandless won nine caps for Ireland, winning his first against England in a 1-1 draw in Belfast in October 1919. He left Rangers in the close season of 1930 to become the player-manager of Ballymena United. In 1934 he became the manager of Dundee but three years later he took charge at Newport County.

He inherited some excellent players and soon developed them into an outstanding combination, guiding them to the Third Division (South) championship in 1938-39. Unfortunately, the war years decimated the Newport County side and Somerton Park was requisitioned by the Army during the hostilities and the club had to close down. In April 1946, McCandless resigned but two months later he became manager of Cardiff City replacing Cyril Spiers.

In his first season at Ninian Park, the Bluebirds won the Third Division (South) championship, finishing seven points clear of their nearest rivals, Queen's Park Rangers.

In November 1947, McCandless joined Swansea Town and in 1948-49 took the Vetch Field club to the Southern Section title. McCandless died in 1955 but he left behind a wealth of talent including the Allchurch brothers, Mel Charles, Cliff Jones and Terry Medwin.

McCULLOCH, ANDY

Starting League football late, Andy McCulloch joined Queen's Park Rangers from Walton and Hersham in 1970. Unable to win a regular place in the Loftus Road club's side, he joined Cardiff City in October 1972 for a fee of £45,000.

He scored on his debut for the Bluebirds in a 3-0 home win over Preston North End and ended the season as the club's top scorer with 14 goals in 26 League games. He also won a Welsh Cup winners' medal as Bangor City were beaten 5-1 on aggregate. He topped the club's scoring charts again in 1973-74 but following the appointment of Jimmy Andrews as manager he was allowed to join Oxford United for a fee of £70,000. He had scored 33 goals in 74 first team games for City but at the Manor Ground he was hampered by a series of niggling injuries and moved on to play for Brentford. His impressive form for the Bees, where he scored 48 goals in 117 League games led to him being signed by Sheffield Wednesday.

In 1979-80, his first season at Hillsborough, his 12 goals in 30 games helped the Owls win promotion to the Second Division. He was the Yorkshire club's top scorer in 1980-81 with 18 goals including a hat-trick in a 4-1 win over Cambridge United. He stayed at Hillsborough until the summer of 1983 when he joined Crystal Palace. In November 1984 he left Selhurst Park and ended his career with Aldershot.

McDOUGALL, DAVY

Signed from Glasgow Rangers, left-half Davy McDougall became Cardiff City's first professional captain in 1910 and assumed the role of player-manager for the 1910-11 season. In that campaign, the club's first in the

Southern League Second Division, McDougall played in 21 games and 17 in the Glamorgan League in which the club also competed. It was a fairly successful season for the Ninian Park club who ended the season in fourth place in the Southern League after being up amongst the promotion contenders for the bulk of the campaign.

In the summer of 1911, Fred Stewart arrived at Ninian Park as the club's first secretary-manager and though McDougall was retained as a player, it soon became evident that he did not figure in the new manager's plans.

Just prior to the start of the 1912-13 season, McDougall accepted an offer from Newport County to become the club's first player-manager.

McLACHLAN, GEORGE

Glasgow-born George McLachlan was one of a small number of footballers to have enjoyed playing League soccer with English, Scottish and Welsh clubs. He began his career by playing junior football with Rutherglen before joining Clyde for the 1922-23 season. His performances for the Scottish club led to a number of Football League clubs making enquiries about the ball-playing outside-left.

In November 1925, McLachlan joined Cardiff City for a fee of £2,000 and made his debut in a 5-2 home win over Leicester City. Despite breaking his leg in 1926, McLachlan bounced back to star in City's 1927 FA Cup winning team, the first and only time the trophy has been won by a non-English club. He was ever-present in 1927-28 but as the Bluebirds dropped towards the Second Division in 1929-30, McLachlan who had scored 25 goals in 166 games for City, joined Manchester United to continue his career in the First Division.

McLachlan had four seasons at Old Trafford, scoring four goals in 116 League and Cup games before moving to join Third Division (North) club, Chester. After only one season with the then Sealand Road club he returned to Scotland to become manager of Queen of the South.

McSEVENEY, JOHNNY

Johnny McSeveney began his career north of the border with Hamilton Academicals but in 1951 he joined Sunderland. In four seasons at Roker Park, McSeveney made only 35 appearances, scoring three goals and when the opportunity came for him to join Cardiff City, he did so. In fact, three Sunderland players joined the Bluebirds in a deal worth £9,000, the others being Harry Kirtley and Howard Sheppeard.

McSeveney made an outstanding debut for City. Playing against his former club Sunderland, he scored twice in a 3-1 win for the Ninian Park club.

In 1956 he scored the winning goal in the Welsh Cup Final when City beat Swansea Town 3-2. The following season he operated at inside-right and in 34 League appearances, scored 12 goals. He had netted 23 goals in 85 first team outings when in 1957 he moved to Somerton Park to join Newport County as part of the deal that brought the Ironsides' Colin Hudson to the Bluebirds.

In four seasons with Newport, McSeveney scored 51 goals in 172 games before moving to play for Hull City where he continued to score on a regular basis, netting 60 goals in 161 league games. After retiring, he coached the Tigers for a short while before becoming manager of Barnsley. Later he was chief coach at Nottingham Forest under Allan Brown but left after the arrival of Brian Clough. He then had a spell as Guyana's national coach and led them to their first win in 29 years before being appointed assistant-manger to Ian Porterfield at both Rotherham United and Sheffield United.

MICALLEF, TARKI
A Welsh Schoolboy international, Tarki Micallef joined Cardiff City as an apprentice and worked his way through the ranks before making his first team debut in a 2-1 defeat at Sheffield United in December 1978. That was his only appearance in the Bluebirds first team that season, and though he

Tarki Micallef

often showed exciting touches, it was not until the 1981-82 season that he established himself as a regular in the City side.

In September 1983 after scoring 11 goals in 81 League games, he left Ninian Park to join Newport County but within twelve months he had moved on to Gillingham. He returned to Cardiff after just two appearances for the Kent club but only made a handful of appearances as the Bluebirds were relegated to the Third Division. At the end of the 1985-86 season he joined Bristol Rovers but after making 18 League appearances for the Pirates, he left to join Barry Town.

MILNE, ALEC

Full-back Alec Milne joined Cardiff City from Arbroath in the summer of 1957 and made his first team debut in a 2-0 home defeat by Middlesbrough on 7 September 1957. By the end of that campaign, Milne had established himself as a first team regular in the Bluebirds' side and in 1958-59 when the club finished ninth in Division Two, he was ever-present. That season also saw the full-back score his only goal for the club as Gloucester City were beaten 3-0 in a Welsh Cup fifth round replay - the Bluebirds going on to win the trophy.

In 1959--60, Milne turned in a number of resolute performances as the club won promotion to the First Division. He was ever-present again in 1961-62, the club's last season in the First Division but then began to suffer from injury problems and after playing the last of his 197 first team games against Plymouth Argyle on 29 August 1964, he left Ninian Park.

He later emigrated to New Zealand and when the Bluebirds toured the sub-continent in the summer of 1968, the Dundee-born defender played against his former club !

MONTGOMERY, STAN

The son-in-law of Jimmy Nelson, he began his career with non-League Romford before joining Hull City during the Second World War. After 'guesting' for Southend United during the 1945-46 season, he returned to Boothferry Park for the first peacetime Football League campaign in 1946-47. After just five League appearances he moved to Southend on a permanent basis. He had two seasons at Roots Hall in which he made 96 League appearances before, on the recommendation of Jimmy Nelson he joined Cardiff City in 1948 for a fee of £6,000.

The giant centre-half scored on his debut in a 2-2 draw at Grimsby Town in January 1949 and played in the remaining 17 League games. He was only on the losing side twice as City finished fourth in the Second Division.

Over the next six seasons, Montgomery missed very few matches and was a tower of strength in the club's promotion-winning season of 1951-52 when his only goal of the campaign secured a point in a 1-1 draw at Notts County.

He went on to play in 260 first team games for the Bluebirds before leaving Ninian Park to play non-League football for Worcester City in 1955. However, his stay was short and he returned to League action with Newport County before playing for Ton Pentre.

He returned to Ninian Park as the club's trainer before becoming Bristol Rovers' South Wales' scout, a position he held for a good number of years. He then became involved with the Bluebirds again when Alan Durban asked him to take charge of the club's triallists.

MOORE, GRAHAM

He began his playing days with Bargoed YMCA in 1956 and joined Cardiff City the following year. After some impressive displays for the Ninian Park club's reserve side, he made his first team debut at Brighton and Hove Albion in September 1958 and scored a last minute equaliser to make the score 2-2.

In 1959-60, Moore scored in the first three games of the season and went on to find the net 13 times in 41 League games as the club won promotion to the First Division. The following season he had the misfortune to break a leg but still managed to score four of City's goals in their 16-0 Welsh Cup win over Knighton. In December 1961, Chelsea manager Tommy Docherty paid £35,000 to take Moore, the 'golden boy' of Welsh Football to Stamford Bridge.

He had scored 32 goals in 101 first team outings for City but in his first few weeks with Chelsea, he struggled to find his form as the club were relegated. He led them back to the top flight in 1962-63 but in November 1963 he was transferred to Manchester United for £35,000.

Unable to make much of an impression at Old Trafford, he moved on to Northampton Town before later playing for Charlton Athletic and Doncaster Rovers. A Welsh international with 21 caps, he won his first against England at Ninian Park in 1960 when he scored with a last minute header to earn his side a 1-1 draw.

MORGAN, RICHIE

Richie Morgan spent ten years at Ninian Park, the majority as understudy to centre-half Don Murray and so only made 69 League appearances.

When his playing days were over, he joined the club's administrative staff before being the surprise choice as manager in November 1978 following the dismissal of Jimmy Andrews.

He surrounded himself with an excellent backroom staff of Dave Elliott, Brian Harris and Doug Livermore, but despite spending money on players such as Dave Bennett, Peter Kitchen and Colin Sullivan, he found little success.

The club brought in Graham Williams as team manager, with Morgan as general manager but both were eventually sacked as the club slid down the table. One of the club's most loyal servants, Morgan became manager of Barry Town and led them to the Welsh League championship on a number of occasions.

MORRIS, TREVOR
After a spell with Ipswich Town, he 'guested' for Cardiff City during the Second World War but his playing career was ended by a broken leg in a game against Bristol City during December 1941.

During the war years, Morris piloted the lead aircraft of a squadron of Lancaster bombers on D-Day and flew in more than 40 missions over enemy territory, for which he was awarded the Distinguished Flying Medal.

He joined Cardiff City as assistant-secretary in 1946 but following Cyril Spiers' resignation he was appointed secretary-manager. Cardiff were relegated from the First Division in 1957 and a year later, he left Ninian Park to work as general manager with Swansea Town.

He took the Swans to the FA Cup semi-final in 1964 but a year later, the Vetch Field club were relegated to the Third Division and Morris resigned his position.

He had a brief spell in charge of Newport County before being appointed secretary of the Welsh FA, a position he held for 11 years.

MOST GOALS IN A SEASON
The club's highest total of goals scored in a season is 93 in 1946-47 when the club won the Third Division (South) championship and were promoted to the Second Division. Stan Richards set a new Club record with 30 goals including a hat-trick in a 6-1 home win over Norwich City.

MOST MATCHES
Cardiff City played their most number of matches, 63, in 1988-89. This comprised 46 League games, three FA Cup games, four Football League

Cup games, three Welsh Cup ties, four European Cup Winners' Cup games and three Sherpa Van Trophy games.

MULLEN, JIMMY

Jimmy Mullen began his career with Sheffield Wednesday, turning professional in 1970. His first season as a regular with the Hillsborough club was 1972-73 but following Wednesday's relegation in 1975, the rest of his career with the Yorkshire club was spent in the Third Division. When he left Hillsborough to join Rotherham United in August 1980 he had played in over 250 senior games for the Owls.

He captained Rotherham to the Third Division championship in 1981 but then joined Cardiff on loan in March 1982 before signing on a permanent basis. He made his debut in a 2-1 defeat at Norwich City and though he turned in some impressive performances in his 12 outings at the end of that season, he failed to prevent the Bluebirds being relegated. In 1982-83 he led the Welsh club to promotion from the Third Division as runners-up to Portsmouth.

After a spell as joint-manager with Jimmy Goodfellow, Mullen became Alan Durban's assistant before being appointed manager on a temporary basis in May 1986. However, after failing to secure the job permanently, Mullen who had played in 154 first team games, joined Newport County as player-manager. After only five months at Somerton Park he joined Aberdeen as assistant-manager to Ian Porterfield. He replaced Sam Ellis as Blackpool manager but his only season at Bloomfield Road ended in relegation. He became manager of Burnley in August 1990 and led the club to nine straight League victories and nine consecutive away wins. In 1991-92 he led the Clarets to the Fourth Division championship. Two years later he led the club to promotion from the new Second Division but after the Turf Moor club lost their First Division status after just one season, Mullen parted company with the club.

MURRAY, DON

One of the greatest centre-halves in the club's history, Don Murray was just 17 years 113 days old when he made his first team debut for the Bluebirds in a 3-2 defeat at Middlesbrough in May 1963. After playing in half of the the club's games the following season, he established himself as the club's first-choice pivot at the start of the 1964-65 campaign, a position he held for 10 seasons.

He was ever-present for three consecutive seasons, 1968-69 to 1970-71

Don Murray tackles Rodney Marsh of QPR in a Division 2 fixture.
Cardiff City 4 QPR 2 - September 27 1969 (Att: 30,083)

and holds the club record for the most consecutive appearances at Football League level when he played in 146 games from 4 May 1968 to 20 November 1971.

Despite often being in trouble with the referees during the early stages of his career, he became a player who led by example and gave his all. The winner of nine Welsh Cup winners' medals during his time at Ninian Park, he was also instrumental in the club reaching the semi-final of the European Cup Winners' Cup in 1967-68. His performances around this time led to offers from the game's top clubs, but Murray remained loyal to Cardiff and though his play was often worthy of full international honours, the Scottish-born centre-half had to be content with just one Under-23 cap.

In October 1974 after appearing in 532 first team games for City he had a five match loan spell with Swansea City before returning north of the border to play for a season with Hearts. He then returned to South Wales to see out his career at Newport County where former Cardiff boss Jimmy Scoular was in charge.

NEAL, PHIL

After beginning his League career with Northampton Town, Phil Neal made 206 first team appearances for the Cobblers before joining LIverpool for £65,000 in October 1974. From his second appearance for the club in December 1974 until injury caused him to miss Liverpool's game with Sunderland in October 1983, Phil Neal played in 366 consecutive League games.

The most capped England right-back with 50 caps to his name, he won almost every honour whilst playing for Liverpool. He won seven League Championship medals and was on the winning side in four League Cup finals. He won a UEFA Cup winners' medal and four European Cup winners' medals - only an FA Cup winners' medal eluded him.

Halfway through the 1985-86 season, he left Anfield to join Bolton Wanderers as player-manager. He led the Trotters to promotion from the Fourth Division and to success in the Sherpa Van Trophy but he left the club at the end of the 1991-92 season. He had brought stability to the club along with a measure of success but poor results and declining attendances prompted his dismissal.

After a period of involvement with the England management team, he took charge of Coventry City before becoming manager of Cardiff City in February 1996. He couldn't wave a magic wand and the Bluebirds finished 22nd in the Third Division. After being replaced by Russell Osman, he went to Manchester City, where he became caretaker-manager following Alan Ball's departure, but was soon replaced by Frank Clark.

NELSON, JIMMY

A member of the famous Scotland 'Wembley Wizards' team, full-back Jimmy Nelson was born in Greenock in 1901. He moved to Ireland with his family and began his football career with Crusaders and captained the Irish Alliance XI that played an England team. He was on the verge of full honours when the Irish found that he was a Scot by birth!

He joined Cardiff in 1921 and made his debut in a goalless draw at West Bromwich Albion in October 1921. After that, he was a virtual fixture in the Bluebirds team and was ever-present in 1923-24 when the club were runners-up in the First Division. In the opening match of the 1925-26 season, Nelson became the first City player to be sent-off in a League match. Playing at Maine Road, he became involved in a last-minute altercation with Manchester City winger Johnson. The referee awarded a penalty to the home side, dismissed Nelson and Cardiff went down 3-2.

He appeared in both City's FA Cup Finals and went on to play in 240 League games for the club before the Cardiff board accepted an offer of £7,000 for him from Newcastle United in the summer of 1930.

He was soon back at Wembley as captain of the Magpies' 1932 FA Cup-winning team. His experience was invaluable in the 2-1 victory over Arsenal. He went on to appear in 159 League games for Newcastle before leaving St James' Park for Southend in June 1935. He played at Roots Hall up until the outbreak of the Second World War and ended his career after playing in 73 League games for them.

Capped four times by Scotland, he assisted Southend for a number of years where his son Tony, an Amateur international played. He later returned to Cardiff and became licensee of the Greyhound Inn.

NEUTRAL GROUNDS

Whilst Ninian Park has been used as a neutral ground for FA Cup matches on a number of occasions, City themselves have had to replay on a neutral ground a number of times.

Date	Opponents	Venue	FA Cup	Score
22.01.1923	Watford	Villa Park	Round 1	2-1
19.01.1925	Darlington	Anfield	Round 1	2-0

16.01.1961	Manchester City	Highbury	Round 3	0-2
15.01.1970	York City	St Andrews	Round 3	1-3
16.02.1972	Sunderland	Maine Road	Round 4	3-1
12.02.1973	Bolton Wanderers	Hawthorns	Round 4	0-1

The club's FA Cup semi-finals were of course played on neutral grounds - Meadow Lane (1924-25) and Molineux (1926-27) - whilst the club's appearances in the FA Cup Final and FA Charity Shield also qualify for inclusion.

NICKNAMES
Because the club's colours are predominantly blue, Cardiff City's nickname is the Bluebirds. Also many players in the club's history have been fondly known by their nickname. They include:

Jack Lewis	1924-1926	'Ginger'
Joe Cassidy	1925-1926	'Trooper'
John Diamond	1935-1936	'Legs'
Jack Prescott	1936-1939	'Pluto'
Charlie Hill	1938-1947	'Midge'
Tommy Best	1948-1949	'Darkie'
Colin Hudson	1957-1961	'Rocky'

NINIAN PARK
In February 1910 the club were offered an area of waste ground which had been used as a rubbish tip, between Sloper Road and the Taff Vale railway. Offered a seven-year lease by the Corporation, the club had to provide guarantees for an annual rent of £90. After one of the club's backers withdrew, Lord Ninian Crichton-Stuart came to the rescue. Thus the ground which was provisionally called Sloper Park, was named in honour of his Lordship's contribution.

Aston Villa, the Football League champions played a friendly at Ninian Park on 1 September 1910 with the official kick-off being performed by Lord Ninian Crichton-Stuart. Approximately 7,000 saw Villa win 2-1 but the honour of scoring Cardiff City's first goal at Ninian Park went to Jack Evans.

A small 200-seat wooden grandstand with a canvas roof was built on the Sloper Road side of the ground with a dressing room erected in the corner. Though the ground was to remain basic for a good number of years, it replaced the Arms Park as Cardiff's football international venue and in March 1911, staged the first game against Scotland.

In 1920 the Canton Stand which was named after the district, was built behind the north goal. After City had won the FA Cup in 1927, the profits of their triumphs funded a second large roof being erected over the Grangetown End terrace in 1928.

On 18 January 1937, the Main Stand was burnt down, the result of thieves trying to blast open the club's safe, which they wrongly believed to contain gate money from the FA Cup tie against Grimsby Town played two days earlier. The old structure was replaced by a stand of brick and steel. The ground remained like this until 1947 when the terrace in front of the Main Stand was extended, and in 1958, the Bob Bank was enlarged and a roof erected over its new rear section. Floodlights were installed in the summer of 1960.

On 14 October 1961, Ninian Park's all-time highest gate was recorded when 61,566 witnessed the Wales v England international.

In 1972-73 the club spent £225,000 on extending the Main Stand to seat nearly 4,500 but in 1977, Ninian Park was designated under the Safety of Sports Ground Act, as a result of which the South Glamorgan authorities reduced the ground's capacity from 46,000 to 10,000 until the repairs were carried out. It cost the club £600,000 of which £200,000 came from the Football Grounds Improvement Trust and £27,000 from the Welsh FA.

Perhaps the most significant of the changes enforced by the Safety Act was the demolition of the Grangetown End roof in 1977 and the cutting down of its banking. As the years unfolded, the Arms Park began to host the majority of international games following doubts about Ninian Park's safety. In 1990 City owed their landlords, Cardiff City Council, for unpaid loan repayments and three areas of the ground had been closed to save policing costs. Ninian Park was by now a sorry state and in February 1991, just 1,629 fans turned up to see City beaten 3-1 by Aldershot.

The club needed a miracle and found one in the form of millionaire Rick Wright, who though he said he didn't like football, put £2 million into the club just 48 hours before a final winding up order.

In late 1991, 2,100 seats were installed on the Main Stand paddock. They were covered by a roof extension, while the terracing under the Bob Bank roof was converted to hold 5,330 seats. At the same time, the Grangetown End was restored for use and the Canton Stand refurbished to allow extra seating for 1,761.

In the summer of 1995, Samesh Kumar took over as chairman of Cardiff City and whilst there are plans to continue the conversion of the remaining terraces to seats, there is also the possibility of the club moving to Cardiff Bay and the involvement of David Sullivan with the Millenium Stadium.

NON-LEAGUE

'Non-League' is the shorthand term for clubs which are not members of the Football League. The Bluebirds have a good record against non-League opposition in the FA Cup competition and have only lost four matches.

The club's record since 1920-21 is:

Date	Opponents	FA Cup	Venue	Score
28.11.1931	Enfield	Round 1	Home	8-0
30.11.1935	Dartford	Round 1	Home	0-3
28.11.1936	Southall	Round 1	Home	3-1
26.11.1938	Cheltenham Town	Round 1	Away	1-1
03.12.1938	Cheltenham Town	Round 1R	Home	1-0
09.01.1954	Peterborough United	Round 3	Home	3-1
13.12.1975	Wycombe Wanderers	Round 2	Home	1-0
20.11.1982	Wokingham Town	Round 1	Away	1-1
23.11.1982	Wokingham Town	Round 1R	Home	3-0
11.12.1982	Weymouth	Round 2	Home	2-3
15.11.1986	Ton Pentre	Round 1	Away	4-1
11.12.1988	Enfield	Round 2	Away	4-1
18.11.1989	Halesowen Town	Round 1	Home	1-0
09.12.1989	Gloucester City	Round 2	Home	2-2
12.12.1989	Gloucester City	Round 2R	Away	1-0
17.11.1990	Hayes	Round 1	Home	0-0
21.11.1990	Hayes	Round 1R	Away	0-1
13.11.1993	Enfield	Round 1	Away	0-0
30.11.1993	Enfield	Round 1R	Home	1-0
11.11.1994	Enfield	Round 1	Away	0-1
11.11.1995	Rushden & Diamonds	Round 1	Away	3-1
16.11.1996	Hendon	Round 1	Home	2-0

NUGENT, CLIFF

Utility forward Cliff Nugent was playing his football with Headington United when Cardiff manager Cyril Spiers brought him to Ninian Park in January 1951. Though he made his debut the following season in a 1-0 home win over Hull City, it was 1953-54 before he began to establish himself in the Bluebirds' first team.

Playing predominantly at inside-right, he scored three League goals in 22 games, his first for City coming in a 3-1 home defeat by Wolverhampton Wanderers on 2 January 1954. The following season he showed his versatility by playing at outside-left, scoring four goals in 24 games as the club just avoided relegation by beating Wolverhampton Wanderers in their final home game.

He missed all but one game of the 1955-56 season through injury before returning for the following campaign, again on the left-wing.

In 1957-58 he scored eight goals in 31 games including a well struck hat-trick in a 7-0 home win over Barnsley.

In November 1958, the London-born Nugent left South Wales to play for Mansfield Town, having scored 23 goals in 133 games spread over eight seasons.

O'FARRELL, FRANK

A regular in the West Ham United side for six years, he gained international recognition, winning the first of seven caps for the Republic of Ireland whilst at Upton Park, against Austria in 1952.

Having made 210 League and Cup appearances for the Hammers, he joined Preston North End and marked his debut for the Deepdale club with a goal against Manchester City. O'Farrell was not on the losing side at North End until his sixteenth game but after a comparatively short association with the club, he moved to non-League Weymouth as player-manager in May 1961.

He proved a success at the south coast club, steering them to the Southern League Championship before taking over at Torquay United, where he gained the club promotion at the end of his first season.

Later when in charge at Leicester City, he led the club to the FA Cup Final and promotion to the First Division before taking over at Manchester United. He found it difficult to follow in the footsteps of Matt Busby and left Old Trafford a bitter man.

He was brought to Ninian Park to replace the recently departed Jimmy Scoular but after only 158 days in charge of the Bluebirds, he left to manage the Iran national team.

He later returned to these shores to manage Torquay United for a second time.

OLDEST PLAYER

The oldest player to line-up in a Cardiff City first team is George Latham. The legendary trainer was 42 years old when he made his one appearance for the club in a 3-1 win at Blackburn Rovers on 2 January 1922.

OSMAN, RUSSELL

Russell Osman began his Football League career with Ipswich Town where he formed an excellent central defensive partnership with Terry Butcher under the managership of Bobby Robson. In 1975 he won an FA Youth Cup winners' medal and after making his debut against Chelsea on 3 September 1977, went on to play in 384 League games for the Portman Road club.

In May 1980 he won the first of 11 full international caps for England when he played against Australia and made his last appearance for his country against Denmark in the European Championship match in September 1983. In between he twice went close to a League Championship medal in 1981 and 1982 when Town finished runners-up in the First Division. He also helped the club win the UEFA Cup in 1981 when they beat AZ67 Alkmaar 5-4 on aggregate. He left Portman Road in the summer of 1985 to join Leicester City for a fee of £240,000 and made 108 League appearances before signing for Southampton for £325,000 in June 1988.

Osman's first managerial role was with Bristol City where he was initially caretaker-manager but in 1994 he lost his job. He became manager of Cardiff City in November 1996 and led the club to seventh place in the Third Division. He was replaced midway through the 1997-98 season by Frank Burrows.

OWN GOALS

Though there have been a number of instances of own goals, Danny Malloy, one of Cardiff City's greatest centre-halves, had an incredible 14 debited to him! Two of them came on the opening day of the 1959-60 season when after Steve Mokone had given City the lead against Liverpool, Malloy put through his own goal twice to give the Reds a 2-1 lead at half-time. Thankfully in the second half, goals from Moore and Watkins gave the Bluebirds a 3-2 win.

One of the most unusual own goals scored by a Cardiff player came from Bobby Woodruff in a 5-0 defeat at Aston Villa on 6 October 1973. The game was only six minutes old when Woodruff who was a full 40 yards from goal, headed past Bill Irwin to put Villa 1-0 up !

P

PENALTIES

On the final day of the 1923-24 season, City needed to beat Birmingham City at St Andrew's to win the League Championship. The game was goalless when with 20 minutes remaining, the Bluebirds were awarded a penalty after Jimmy Gill's goalbound header was punched away by a Birmingham defender. Both Jack Evans and Jimmy Gill were reluctant to take the spot-kick so it was Len Davies who stepped forward. He shot straight at the Birmingham 'keeper Tremelling and the game ended goalless. Huddersfield Town beat Nottingham Forest 3-0 to win the title on goal average.

On 17 April 1954, Alf Sherwood who had replaced Ron Nicholls in goal, saved a penalty from Liverpool's Billy Liddell in front of the Kop in a 1-0 win for City at Anfield.

City goalkeeper Ken Jones was almost late arriving for the game against Bristol Rovers on 26 March 1958 because he had been engrossed in the FA Cup semi-final between Fulham and Manchester United on the television. City lost 2-0 to record their first home defeat in 12 games. Jones was dropped to the club's Welsh League XI but responded by scoring from the penalty-spot in a 2-1 win over Haverfordwest.

When the Bluebirds entertained Hull City on 29 August 1973, they were awarded a penalty. Gary Bell, who gave away two penalties on his debut, took the spot-kick. His shot was saved by Jeff Wealands but the ball looped up and Bell following up, headed into an empty net and so became only the sixth player in the history of the Football League to be credited with a headed penalty !

PERRY, JASON

Newport-born Jason Perry made his debut for the Ninian Park club in a goalless draw at home to Exeter City in March 1987, though it was 1989-90 before he established himself as a regular first team member.

After winning Under-21 and 'B' international honours, the strong tackling defender was capped at full level when he played against Norway in 1994. After helping the club win promotion in 1992-93, he hardly missed a game until 1995-96 when he suffered the worst injury crisis of his career. He bounced back the following season and missed very few games in helping the Bluebirds to the play-offs. After spending almost 10 years at Ninian Park and appearing in 344 first team games, he was offered a free transfer and left the club to join Bristol Rovers.

Jason Perry

PETHARD, FREDDIE

Glasgow-born full-back Freddie Pethard began his career with Celtic but after failing to make the grade, was released in 1969. After joining Cardiff City he worked his way up through the ranks and finally got his chance in the first team in March 1972 when he played in a 1-1 home draw against Oxford United.

Pethard was able to play in both full-back positions and so provided cover for City's regular pairing of Carver and Bell. By 1974-75, Pethard had established himself in the Bluebirds' first team at left-back and went on to play in 203 first team games in eight seasons at Ninian Park, all this despite being hampered by a series of injuries. His only goals at first team level came in the Welsh Cup Final against Hereford United in 1976 and Shrewsbury Town in 1977.

Following the arrival of Colin Sullivan in February 1979, Pethard left Ninian Park and joined Torquay United where he appeared in 105 League games.

PHILLIPS, LEIGHTON

A Welsh Schoolboy international, Leighton Phillips made his Cardiff City debut as a substitute in a 2-2 draw at home to Rotherham United in January 1968. He scored with his first touch of the ball to draw City level after they had been two goals down. Though he played in a handful of games over the next few seasons, it was 1970-71 before he established himself in the Bluebirds' first team.

His performances as a defensive sweeper led to him winning Welsh Under-21 and Under-23 caps before he won the first of 56 full caps when he played against Czechoslovakia in 1971. He went on to play in 216 first team games for Cardiff and was ever-present in 1972-73.

In September 1974 he joined Aston Villa for a fee of £100,000. In his first season with the club, he helped Villa to win promotion to the First Division as runners-up to Manchester United. He won a League Cup winners' tankard in 1977 as Villa beat Everton but the following year, the versatile performer who played in 175 games for Villa, was sold to Swansea City. After three years at the Vetch Field in which he helped the Swans win promotion twice, he had a short spell with Charlton Athletic before ending his career as a non-contract player with Exeter City.

PIKE, CHRIS

Centre-forward Chris Pike played his early football in the Cardiff Combination League before playing Welsh League football, first for Maesteg and then Barry Town. After some impressive performances, he was given his chance in the Football League by Fulham. He did well in his first season at Craven Cottage but then after an arm injury, failed to regain his place.

He joined his home-town team Cardiff City on loan and made his debut in a 2-0 home win over Aldershot. After returning to Craven Cottage, he rejoined the Bluebirds on a permanent basis, having scored four goals in 42 League games for the London club.

He became a much more prolific scorer at Ninian Park and in 1989-90, despite the club being relegated, scored 18 goals in 41 League games. He also netted five goals in cup games to take his season's tally to 23. He continued to find the net in his stay at Cardiff and in 1991-92 had his best season in terms of goals scored when he netted 21 in 40 League games, including a hat-trick in a 5-0 home win over Wrexham.

Pike went on to score 67 League goals for the club in 154 outings before leaving to join Hereford United. He later signed for Gillingham where he ended his League career.

PITCH
The Ninian Park pitch measures 114 yards by 78 yards.

PLASTIC
There have been four Football League clubs that replaced their normal grass playing pitches with artificial surfaces at one stage or another. Queen's Park Rangers were the first in 1981 but the Loftus Road plastic was discarded in 1988 in favour of a return to turf. Luton Town, Oldham Athletic and Preston North End followed.

The Bluebirds have never played on the Luton or Oldham plastic but went down 2-0 on 28 November 1981 on Queen's Park Rangers' Loftus Road plastic, the only occasion they played on it. Cardiff have played on North End's Deepdale plastic on three occasions. A Mike Ford goal gave City a 1-0 win on 4 November 1986 whilst goals from Gilligan and Bartlett (2) helped them secure a point in an exciting 3-3 draw in 1988-89. City's last visit to play on the Deepdale plastic on 24 February 1990 saw them go down 4-0.

PLATNAUER, NICKY
Nicky Platnauer was working as a bank clerk when Bedford Town folded and was surprisingly signed by Bristol Rovers. He impressed them so much that Rovers' boss Bobby Gould took him to Coventry City when he became manager at Highfield Road. He proved a disappointment in the First Division and Ron Saunders bought him to play wide on the left in Birmingham City's bid for promotion. Things didn't work out for him at St Andrews and after a loan spell at Reading he joined Cardiff City in September 1986.

He made his debut for the Bluebirds in a 1-1 draw at Halifax Town and went on to be a virtual ever-present for the club over the next three seasons, scoring nine goals in 147 games. In 1987-88 he helped the club win promotion to the

Third Division and win the Welsh Cup after beating Wrexham 2-0 in the final. After leaving Cardiff he played for Notts County before joining Port Vale on loan. He later played for Leicester City, Scunthorpe United and Mansfield Town before playing for Bedworth United.

PLAY-OFFS

After finishing seventh in the Nationwide Third Division in 1996-97, City qualified for the play-offs for the first time in their history. A crowd of 11,369 saw Northampton Town win the first leg of the semi-final at Ninian Park with a Sean Parrish goal. In the second leg at the Sixfields Stadium, Jason Fowler pulled a goal back for City after Sampson had extended Northampton's aggregate lead to 2-0. Further goals from Warburton and Gayle put the Cobblers in a commanding position before Simon Haworth reduced the arrears in the last minute.

POINTS

Under the three points for a win system which was introduced in 1981-82, Cardiff City's best tally is 86 points gained in 1982-83 when the club finished runners-up in the Third Division and were promoted. However, the club's best points haul under the old two points for a win system was 66 points in 1946-47 when they won the Third Division (South) championship. This would have netted them 96 points under the present system. Cardiff's worst record under either system was the meagre 24 points secured in 1933-34 when the club finished bottom of the Third Division (South).

PONTIN, KEITH

A one club man, centre-half Keith Pontin worked his way up through the ranks before making his first team debut in a 2-0 win at Charlton Athletic on the opening day of the 1976-77 season. Following the arrival of Paul Went from Portsmouth, he went back to playing reserve team football before being recalled to the first team in September 1977 after Went was moved into attack.

Over the next four seasons, the Pontyclun-born defender missed very few matches and his form was such that he won two full caps for Wales, the first against England in 1980.

During the 1981-82 season when the club were relegated from the Second Division, Pontin played in 40 matches, more than anyone else. One of the club's most experienced players at that time, he left Ninian Park during the early part of the following season after an argument with City manager Len Ashurst. Pontin, who had played in 231 first team games for the Bluebirds was aged just 26 when he joined Merthyr Tydfil in the Southern League. He later signed for Barry Town, playing out his career with the successful Welsh League club.

POSTPONED

The bleak winter of 1962-63, described at the time as the 'Modern Ice Age' proved to be one of the most chaotic seasons in British soccer. The worst Saturday for League action in that awful winter was 9 February when only seven Football League fixtures went ahead.

The worst Saturday for the FA Cup was 5 January, the day of the third round when only three of the 32 ties could be played. The Bluebirds' tie at Charlton Athletic had to be postponed 14 times and was eventually played on 18 February 1963 with the home side winning 1-0 courtesy of a Len Glover goal, a few minutes from time.

PROMOTION

The Bluebirds have been promoted on eight occasions. They were first promoted in 1920-21 at the end of their first season in the Football League when they finished runners-up to Birmingham on goal average. Following eight seasons in the First Division, the club suffered two relegations in the space of three seasons before spending nine seasons in the Third Division.

The club's second experience of promotion came in 1946-47, the first season of peacetime football following the Second World War. The Blue-birds won the Third Division (South) championship, finishing nine points clear of runners-up Queen's Park Rangers. They were promoted for a third time in 1951-52 when they won their last six home games to finish runners-up behind Sheffield Wednesday and so return to the top flight. After five seasons in the First Division, City were relegated only to win promotion in their third season back in the Second Division when they finished one point adrift of champions, Aston Villa.

Cardiff then spent two seasons in the First Division before being relegated to the Second Division. After 13 seasons the club dropped into the Third Division but were promoted after just one season when they finished runners-up to Hereford United. Following relegation in 1981-82, City again won promotion at the first time of asking, finishing five points behind champions Portsmouth in an exciting Third Division campaign. The club's seventh experience of promotion came in their second season of Fourth Division football when they joined Wolverhampton Wanderers and Bolton in moving up to a higher grade of football. They were last promoted in 1992-93 when they won the first championship of the 'new' Third Division following reorganisation by the Football League.

Cardiff City team photograph
May 5th 1976
Back row, (left to right): Fred Pethard, Doug Livermore, Ron Healey, Brian Clark, Keith Pontin, Derek Showers, John Buchanan, Tony Villars, Willie Anderson, Albert Larmour, Phil Dwyer. (Front): David Giles, Peter Sayer, Richie Morgan, Tony Evans, Adrian Alston, Clive Charles, Alan Campbell, Brian Attley.

PUGH, REG

Cardiff-born Reg Pugh was just 17 years old when he made his debut for the Bluebirds in a 3-1 win at Watford on 20 October 1934, thus becoming one of the club's youngest debutants.

The speedy winger soon established himself in the City side and in 1935-36 when the club finished 20th in the Third Division (South) he was an ever-present. Though not a prolific scorer, he netted five goals in the first seven matches of the following season and went on to score 31 goals in 191 first team games up until the outbreak of the Second World War. In the last League season prior to the hostilities, Pugh had lost his place to new signings Albert Rhodes and Tom Rickards but soon bounced back with such great effect that both Rhodes and Rickards were allowed to leave Ninian Park. Pugh played for Cardiff City up until 1941.

Q

QUICKEST GOALS

The club's records do not include precise goals times since 1910 and so it is an impossible task to state accurately the club's quickest goalscorer. Certainly one of the quickest was Trevor Ford's 15 second strike in City's 4-1 defeat at Charlton Athletic on 23 October 1954. Andy McCulloch netted after 18 seconds in Cardiff's 1-1 draw at Fulham on 31 March 1973.

R

RECEIPTS

The club's record receipts are £141,756 for the FA Cup fourth round match against Manchester City on 29 January 1994 which the Bluebirds won 1-0 through a Nathan Blake goal.

REECE, GIL

Gil Reece joined Cardiff City as a part-timer whilst continuing his trade as a plumber. He graduated to the club's reserve side and had a loan spell with Welsh League Ton Pentre but towards the end of the 1962-63 season he was released and left to see out the season with Pembroke Borough. After turning in some useful displays, he was offered the chance to join Newport County and in 1964-65 he became one of the club's most consistent goalscorers.

At the end of that season he joined Sheffield United for a fee of £10,000 and his performances during the early part of the 1965-66 campaign led to him winning his first Welsh cap against England at Ninian Park. Apart from minor injuries he held his place in the Welsh side for the next few seasons, winning 29 caps until he suffered a broken leg against Blackpool whilst playing for the Blades. He went on to score 58 goals in 210 appearances for the Bramall Lane club before leaving to join Cardiff City in September 1972.

He became club captain and played in a variety of roles for the Welsh club and in his first season, scored a hat-trick in a 5-0 second leg Welsh

Cup Final win over Bangor City. He repeated the feat the following season when he scored the only goal of the Welsh Cup Final second leg against Stourbridge. Though the club were relegated in 1974-75, Reece was the top scorer with nine League goals. The following season he helped the Bluebirds win promotion to the Second Division at the first attempt and won his third Welsh Cup winners' medal. He had scored 35 goals in 114 games for City before returning to the Vetch Field for a short spell.

RE-ELECTION
Cardiff City have had to apply for re-election to the Football League on just one occasion and that was in 1933-34 when they finished bottom of the Third Division (South). The City defence conceded 105 goals including defeats against Gillingham (Away 2-6), Swindon Town (Away 3-6), Bristol City (Home 1-5) and Bristol Rovers (Home 1-5). Fortunately, they were immediately re-elected at the Football League AGM.

REES, BILLY
A coalminer for seven years, Billy Rees was playing for Caernarfon Rovers when spotted by Cardiff City manager Cyril Spiers. Principally an inside-forward, Rees was capable of playing in any of the forward positions. He turned out regularly for the Bluebirds during the Second World War, playing in 83 games and scoring 74 goals and played for Wales against England in a wartime international.

He was a regular member of the Cardiff side that won the Third Division (South) championship in 1946-47, scoring 16 goals in 35 League appearances. He was the club's top scorer the following season with 11 goals but in the summer of 1949, after netting 33 goals in 101 League games, he left Ninian Park to join Tottenham Hotspur. Just before he left the Bluebirds, he won the first of three full Welsh caps against Northern Ireland in March 1949.

Early on at White Hart Lane, he suffered from a series of minor injuries and consequently didn't make his debut until December 1949. During that promotion-winning season, Rees played in just 14 games and at the end of the campaign, he left to sign for Leyton Orient. In just over five years at Brisbane Road he netted 66 goals in 198 appearances before moving into non-League circles with Headington United and Kettering Town.

RELEGATION
Cardiff City have been relegated on 10 occasions with their first experi-

ence coming in 1928-29 when after eight seasons of First Division football, City finished bottom of the League, despite conceding the fewest goals. Their second taste of relegation came in 1930-31 when after beginning the season with five straight defeats, they never recovered and finished bottom of the Second Division. City's third experience of relegation came in 1956-57 following two promotions.

Winning only one of their last 14 matches, they dropped into the Second Division with Charlton Athletic. Three seasons later they won promotion, but in 1961-62 the club played their last season of top flight football when along with Chelsea they were relegated to the Second Division.

The club then spent 13 seasons in this division before being relegated for a fifth time in 1974-75. The Bluebirds won instant promotion but in 1981-82 they were relegated again despite the managerial changes. Again the club only spent one season in the Third Division before winning promotion but two seasons later they were relegated for a seventh time. In 1985-86 the club were relegated for a second successive season and spent two seasons in the League's basement before returning to the Third Division.

The club were relegated for a ninth time in 1989-90 following their worst-ever start to a season when a 3-2 win at Huddersfield Town was their only success in the opening 14 games. City's tenth and final experience of relegation came in 1994-95 when they finished 22nd in the Second Division.

RICHARDS, STAN

Though he was born in Cardiff, Stan Richards played his early football in London with Tufnell Park before returning to South Wales to play for Cardiff Corries. Billy McCandless was alerted and in the summer of 1946, Richards joined Cardiff City. He scored on his Football League debut in a 2-1 defeat at Norwich City, the first of 30 League goals in that 1946-47 season. His total which included a hat-trick in a 6-1 home win over the Canaries on 28 December 1946, is still the club record for the most League goals by an individual in a season.

He was a great favourite with the Cardiff crowd who would often shout 'Open the score Richards and nod one in', illustrating the impact he had made in such a short space of time.

Surprisingly, he only won one Welsh cap and that was against England in 1947. In 1947-48 he tended to suffer from a series of niggling injuries and at the end of that season in which he had scored 39 goals in just 57 League games, he was allowed to join his former manager Billy McCandless at Swansea Town. Though he was still experiencing problems with his knee, he scored 26 goals in 32 games for the Vetch Field club to help them win the Third Division (South) championship in 1948-49.

ROBBINS, WALTER

A skilful, forceful front runner, Walter Robbins joined Cardiff City from his home-town club Ely United and after impressing George Latham in the club's reserve side, he made his first team debut in what was the club's only away win of the season, a 1-0 victory at Portsmouth on 8 December 1928. At the end of that campaign the Bluebirds were relegated but Robbins had turned in a number of outstanding performances and was included in the Welsh FA Party to tour Canada in the close season.

Playing at both inside and outside left, he settled down to be a regular member of the Cardiff side and in October 1930 won his first full cap for Wales when he played in a 1-1 draw against Scotland at Hampden Park. From then on, he became an automatic choice and helped Wales win the International Championship two years running in 1932-33 and 1933-34.

In 1931-32, Robbins scored 21 goals in 34 League games including a hat-trick in a 5-1 home win over Reading and five goals against Thames Association in the club's record 9-2 League win. However, by April of that season, he was a West Bromwich Albion player, as the Welsh club pursued their policy of selling off their better young players.

At the Hawthorns he linked up with Jimmy Murphy and England international Wally Boyes and though he was to enjoy eight seasons with the Baggies, his one disappointment was that he should be missing from their 1935 FA Cup Final line-up. A combination of injury and poor form meant that he didn't play in as many games as he should have and after netting 26 goals in 85 games for Albion, he joined Newport County for the 1939-40 season of War League football.

After the hostilities he joined Cardiff City as a member of the coaching staff. He later did the same job for Newport County and Swansea as well as being appointed the national team's trainer.

RODGERSON, IAN

Hereford-born Ian Rodgerson suffered an early setback in his career when he was not taken on as an apprentice with his home-town club simply because the Edgar Street club had axed its youth team. Later he was given a second chance by Hereford and developed into a useful midfielder, playing wide on the right and being ever eager to support his forwards. He had played in 119 games for Hereford when Cardiff paid £35,000 for his services in the summer of 1988.

He made his debut at right-back in a 4-0 beating at Bolton Wanderers and held his place for most of the season, playing in 39 games. In 1989-90 he missed just one game of the club's relegation season and was one of a small number of City players to turn in consistent displays throughout the campaign. In December 1990 he left Ninian Park and joined Birmingham City for £50,000. He had made 116 first team appearances for the St Andrews club when in the summer of 1993, Sunderland splashed out £140,000 to take him to Roker Park.

He suffered from injuries and a loss of form and after making just 10 League appearances in two seasons, was given a free transfer and returned to Cardiff for a second spell. He took his total number of first team appearances for the Bluebirds to 192 before being released at the end of the 1996-97 season.

RODRIGUES, PETER

A former Welsh Schoolboy and Youth international, Peter Rodrigues was introduced to League football by his home-town club, Cardiff City. He made his debut in a 3-3 draw at Sunderland in September 1963, a match in which Ivor Allchurch scored a hat-trick for the Bluebirds. After that he never looked back and was a virtual ever-present, playing in both full-back positions. In December 1965, Rodrigues, who had won the first of 40 Welsh caps against Northern Ireland earlier that year, joined Leicester City for £45,000.

In 1968-69 the Filbert Street club were relegated to the Second Division but also reached the FA Cup Final where they lost to Manchester City. His performances for the Filberts led to him being wanted by a number of top-flight clubs, but in October 1970 he joined Second Division Sheffield Wednesday for £50,000. He failed to prevent the Hillsborough club from being relegated and in the 1975 close season he joined Southampton.

His career had a fairy tale ending as he captained the Saints to victory over Manchester United in the FA Cup Final of 1976.

RONSON, BILLY

A diminutive, tigrish midfield player, Fleetwood-born Billy Ronson began his League career with his local club Blackpool, and made his first team debut for the Seasiders in a goalless home draw against Nottingham Forest in March 1975. Over the next five years he scored 13 goals in 145 League and Cup games for the Bloomfield Road club before Cardiff City paid a record £130,000 for his services in the summer of 1979.

After making his Bluebirds debut in a 4-1 defeat at Notts County on the opening day of the 1979-80 season, he went on to miss just one game as the club finished 15th in the Second Division. In 1980-81 he was the club's only ever-present but just seven games into the following season he left Ninian Park, being sold to Wrexham for £90,000.

After just one season at the Racecourse Ground in which the Robins were relegated to the Third Division, he left to join Barnsley for £50,000. Highly rated by the Yorkshire club, he appeared in 113 League games over the next three seasons but following a disagreement with manager Allan Clarke, he was allowed to leave Oakwell and after a loan spell at Birmingham City, he returned to Blackpool as a non-contract player.

Unable to capture his best form, he left to play for Baltimore Blasts, becoming one of the most successful performers on the American indoor circuit.

RUGBY LEAGUE

During the summer of 1981, Cardiff City Blue Dragons Rugby League Club was formed under the managership of David Watkins and were to play their home games at Ninian Park. They stayed at the home of the Bluebirds for three seasons but attendances were only averaging 600 and they left to play at Bridgend.

It was a great relief to City supporters who believed that not only was the playing surface at Ninian Park being damaged but that no funds had been made available to strengthen the football team.

RUNNERS-UP

The Bluebirds have been runners-up in a divisional championship on seven occasions - Division One (1923-24), Division Two (1920-21, 1951-52 and 1959-60), Division Three (1975-76 and 1982-83) and Division Four (1987-88).

RUTTER, CHARLIE

London-born full-back Charlie Rutter joined Cardiff City from non-League Taunton Town in September 1949 but had to wait over a year before making his Football League debut for the Bluebirds. It came in a goalless draw at Doncaster Rovers on 21 October 1950.

He was an important member of the City side that won promotion to the First Division in 1951-52, his outstanding defensive displays earning him a call up to the England 'B' side. A knee injury sustained in the 1-0 home win over Notts County towards the end of that season kept him out of the entire 1952-53 campaign in the top flight. When he had recovered his fitness he faced stiff competition from Ron Stitfall and in August 1958 after appearing in 133 first team games for the Bluebirds, he joined Exeter City.

S

SAYER, PETER

Local-born forward Peter Sayer worked his way up through the club's junior ranks before making his debut for the Bluebirds in a 2-1 home defeat by Hull City in September 1974. He went on to play in nine League games that season and scored his first goal for the club in a 1-0 home win over Portsmouth. He missed the last game of that season after breaking an ankle at Southampton on 22 April 1975. He recovered to play in a number of matches towards the end of the 1975-76 season as the club won promotion to the Second Division.

Next season, Sayer missed just a handful of matches as the club finished 18th in Division Two, his form winning him the first of seven full Welsh international caps when he played against Czechoslovakia. Towards the end of that campaign, Sayer who wasn't a prolific scorer, found the net six times in six games.

Midway through the 1977-78 season he left Ninian Park to join Brighton and Hove Albion for £100,000. In his first season at the Goldstone Ground, he helped the Seagulls win promotion to the First Division before later moving to play for Preston North End.

He returned to Cardiff on loan in September 1981, playing in just four games and scoring in a 3-2 win at Luton Town. He left the Welsh club after scoring 20 goals in 98 first team outings to end his League career with Chester before appearing in non-League football for Northwich Victoria.

Peter Sayer

SCOULAR, JIMMY

The son of a miner, Jimmy Scoular became a steel-foundry worker on leaving school, though he always had a keen interest in football. He won junior caps for Scotland before joining the Royal Navy in 1943. He was posted 500 miles away from home to HMS Dolphin near Portsmouth. He played for Gosport Borough and for the Navy team. In December 1945 he signed professional forms for Portsmouth but could not devote his attentions to full-time football until his demobilisation a year later.

For almost seven seasons he was part of a great half-back line of Scoular - Flewin - Dickinson, the backbone of Portsmouth's League Championship victories of 1949 and 1950. He won nine Scottish caps while at Fratton Park but after appearing in 264 League and Cup games for Pompey, he moved to Newcastle United for £22,250. Appointed captain, he skippered the Magpies to Wembley in 1955 and helped them bring the FA Cup to Tyneside for the third time in five seasons. He had played in 271 League and Cup games for Newcastle when he accepted the player-manager's job at Bradford Park Avenue. He took them to Division Three only to be relegated two years later.

He finally hung up his boots in March 1964 and later that year became manager of Cardiff City, a position he filled for nine years. He was unlucky never to win anything other than seven Welsh Cup Finals, although he did take the club to the semi-finals of the European Cup Winners' Cup in 1967-68. He turned the Bluebirds into one of the best sides in the Second Division but in 1973 following boardroom changes, he was sacked. A brief stay with Newport County followed until he left the manager's merry-go-round in January 1978.

SEARLE, DAMON

After making his first team debut for the Bluebirds in a 4-0 Leyland Daf Cup defeat at Shrewsbury Town in December 1989, the Cardiff-born left-back played his first League game in a 1-1 home draw against Peterborough United on 27 October 1990. He went on to appear in all the remaining 34 League games that season before becoming the club's only ever-present in 1991-92. That season also saw him score his first goal for the club in a 2-1 home win over Walsall after the Bluebirds had come from behind.

In six seasons at Ninian Park, Searle was a virtual ever-present and appeared in 285 first team games.

Representing Wales at Youth, Under-21 and 'B' international level, he was monitored by Welsh boss Bobby Gould but failed to win full honours. He left Ninian Park in May 1996 to join Stockport County on a free transfer.

After losing his place to Lee Todd, he regained it in 1997-98, following the Stockport defender's move to Southampton.

SECOND DIVISION

Cardiff City have had eight spells in the Second Division. Their first was their initial League season, 1920-21. At the end of that season they finished second to Birmingham and were promoted to the First Division. They survived eight seasons of top flight football, finishing second in 1923-24 before sliding back into the Second Division. After two seasons the Bluebirds were relegated to the Third Division (South) after losing the first five matches of the 1930-31 season. Their third experience of Second Division football lasted five seasons from 1947-48 before the club were promoted to the top flight in 1951-52. It had been an eventful five seasons in which the club also finished third, fourth and fifth. Following relegation in 1956-57, City's fourth spell in the Second Division lasted three seasons before they won promotion in 1959-60, scoring 90 goals in the process as they finished runners-up to Aston Villa.

Cardiff City 1 Birmingham 1 - September 18th 1920 - Second Division match (Att: 45,000)

Back (from left): Billy Hardy, Dr. Alex Brownlee, Jack Page (twelfth man), Sid Nicholls (director),
Bert Smith, Fred Stewart (Secretary/Manager), Jack Kneeshaw, E. Lewis Williams (director),
Charlie Brittan (Captain), Walter Parker (director), Fred Keenor.
Front (from left): Billy Grimshaw, Jimmy Gill, Arthur Cashmore, George West, Jack Evans, Albert Barnett.

The club's next spell in the Second Division lasted 13 seasons and is their longest in any division of the Football League. During this spell the club struggled to avoid relegation before succumbing to the inevitable in 1974-75. After just one season in the Third Division, the Bluebirds embarked on their sixth spell in the Second Division in 1976-77. Their stay of six seasons saw them continually battle against relegation until they dropped into the Third Division in 1981-82. After gaining promotion, Cardiff began their seventh spell in the Second Division in 1983-84 with hope of promotion but two seasons later they had been relegated and were again the following season, to move into the League's basement for the first time in their history.

The club's last spell in the Second Division followed after winning the Third Division championship after reorganisation, and lasted two seasons before relegation in 1994-95.

SEMI-FINALS
Up until the end of the 1997-98 season, the Bluebirds had been in three FA Cup semi-finals, one League Cup semi-final and in 1967-68 reached the semi-finals of the European Cup Winners' Cup. On top of winning the Welsh Cup 21 times, the club have appeared in a total of 42 semi-finals.

SHERPA VAN TROPHY
The Sherpa Van Trophy replaced the Freight Rover Trophy, and in 1987-88 the Bluebirds beat Wrexham 3-2 in their opening match before going down 3-1 at Walsall. However, they still managed to qualify for the knock-out stages on goal difference. In the first round they travelled to Notts County but went out of the competition 2-0.

In the following season, goals from Curtis and Gilligan gave City a 2-0 home win over Swansea City and though they lost 3-1 at Torquay United they still qualified for the knockout stages where they lost 2-1 at Bristol Rovers with Paul Wimbleton netting for the Bluebirds.

SHERWOOD, ALF
During the early years of the Second World War Alf Sherwood played for Aberdare Town and Aberaman. It was whilst playing against Cardiff City in a War League game that he impressed the Ninian Park club, and he signed for them in 1941. Having been switched from half-back to full-back, he appeared in 140 wartime games for the Bluebirds before making his Football League debut in a 2-1 defeat at Norwich City on the opening day

of the 1946-47 season. He missed just one game that season as City won the Third Division (South) championship.

Having played for Wales in a Victory international against Ireland, it came as no surprise when he won his first full cap against England at Manchester in 1946. Over the next six years he hardly missed an international and won 41 caps. He also had a spell as captain of the team including the famous win over England in 1955.

After Fred Stansfield had left Ninian Park to join Newport County, Alf Sherwood was given the captaincy of the team. He was ever-present in 1949-50 and in 1951-52 led the side to promotion to the First Division.

The master of the sliding tackle, he was also a stand-in goalkeeper for both Cardiff City and Wales. When the Bluebirds travelled to Anfield for an end of season in game in April 1954, the home side had to win to keep their First Division status. Sherwood had taken over in goal following an injury to Ron Howells and faced a penalty from Scottish international Billy Liddell. He saved it and Liverpool were relegated ! He replaced the injured Jack Kelsey for Wales against England at Wembley in 1956, and though he made some outstanding saves, Wales lost 3-1.

At the end of the 1955-56 season, after he had played in 383 first team games, he left to join Newport County, where he scored 21 goals in 205 games before becoming manager of Barry Town.

Cardiff City 1 Leyton Orient 0 - June 7th 1947

Back (from left): K. Hollyman, Bob Allison (trainer), S. Richards, D. Canning, G. Williams, W. Rees, B. Allen, R. Clarke.
Second row: C. Gibson, A. Lever, F. Stansfield, Alf Sherwood, G. Wardle. Seated in front: W. Baker, D. Ross.

SLOAN, TOM

Centre-half Tom Sloan played his early football with Belfast Crusaders before joining Irish League side Linfield. He signed for Cardiff City in the summer of 1924 and made his League debut in a 1-1 draw at home to Notts County in February 1925. In his first couple of seasons at Ninian Park, he was in competition for the number five shirt with Fred Keenor but when the Bluebirds won the FA Cup in 1927, both Keenor and Sloan were in the Cardiff side. Also that season he won a Welsh Cup winners' medal when Rhyl were beaten 2-0 in the final.

Though he only made 97 appearances during five seasons at Ninian Park, he won eight full international caps for Ireland, the first against Scotland in 1926.

His only goal for the club came against City's opponents in the 1927 Final, Arsenal in a 1-1 draw in November 1928.

After leaving Ninian Park he returned to Ireland to rejoin Linfield where he added an Irish Cup winners' medal to his collection. On his retirement from the game he became manager of his home-town club, Portadown.

SMALLEST PLAYER

Although such statistics are always unreliable, the distinction of being Cardiff City's smallest player must go to Willie Carlin and Brian Flynn both of whom stand 5ft 4ins.

SMITH, ERNEST 'BERT'

One of the greatest defenders in the history of Cardiff City, Irish international Bert Smith played his early football for the Indian Army during the First World War before joining the Bluebirds prior to the start of the 1919-20 season. During that campaign he played in more Southern League games than anyone else and was instrumental in the club finishing fourth in that competition's First Division. His only goal that season and the first of three he scored for the club came in a 3-1 win over Newport County.

He made his Football League debut in the club's first-ever game at Stockport County and over the next three seasons was a virtual ever-present in the City side. After the club had won promotion at the end of the 1920-21 season, Smith scored the club's first goal in Division One when they went down 2-1 at Aston Villa.

He won four full caps for Ireland, the first against Scotland in 1921. He had appeared in 146 first team games in all competitions when towards the end of the 1923-24 season, he joined Middlesbrough. However, his opportunities were limited and after just 21 outings he joined Watford who were managed by former Cardiff centre-forward Fred Pagnam. He played in 50 games for the Hornets before hanging up his boots.

SOUTHERN LEAGUE

Cardiff City were admitted to the Second Division of the Southern League in 1910 and played their inaugural match in the competition on 24 September 1910 when they beat Ton Pentre 4-1 at Ninian Park with goals from Bob Peake (2) Billy Watt and Jack Evans. City went on to have a successful season, ending their first campaign in the Southern League in fourth place.

Two of their best results came away from Ninian Park when they won 7-4 at Kettering and 7-1 at Chesham where Bob Peake scored four goals and Jack Evans a hat-trick.

In 1911-12, City opened the season with a 3-1 home win over Kettering Town and as the campaign wore on, they looked likely to win a promotion place. However, two defeats in consecutive games - Portsmouth (Away 2-3) and Merthyr Tydfil (Home 1-2) saw City settle for third place behind Pompey and champions Merthyr who were both promoted.

Cardiff opened their 1912-13 season at the Vetch Field in what was Swansea's first-ever Southern League game. Jack Burton scored for City in a 1-1 draw. The club were unbeaten until the 12th game of the season when they lost 2-0 at Luton Town on Boxing Day. It was City's only defeat of the season as they bounced back to beat Llanelli 5-0 and Ton Pentre 9-0 and go on to win promotion and the championship with ease.

Manager Fred Stewart decided to stick with his championship-winning side of the previous season for the 1913-14 season in the First Division of the Southern League. After losing 1-0 at Bristol Rovers in their opening match, City failed to win a game until their seventh match of the season, when they beat Watford 2-0. A final placing of 10th was a satisfactory performance.

There was a marked improvement in 1914-15 when the Bluebirds finished third in the Southern League First Division. In a game in which every Cardiff forward was on the scoresheet, Bristol Rovers were beaten 7-0 and though they were almost invincible at home, winning 16 of their 19 matches, their away form let them down.

The club's final season in the Southern League was 1919-20 when they produced a mid-season run of 15 games without defeat to end the campaign in fourth place.

SPIERS, CYRIL

An agile and brave goalkeeper, he began his career with Aston Villa. He had made over 100 first team appearances when he was injured towards the end of the 1926-27 season and Villa decided he would not be fit to play again and released him. However, he underwent an experimental operation during the close season and was signed by Tottenham Hotspur.

At White Hart Lane he represented the Football League and played in the international trial match of March 1931 but after 186 games for Spurs he was given a free transfer. He then became assistant-manager to Major Frank Buckley at Wolverhampton Wanderers before taking on the manager's role at Cardiff City.

The outbreak of the Second World War spoiled his rebuilding programme and though he stayed with the Bluebirds throughout the hostilities, he left his post in 1946 to join Norwich City in a similar capacity. At the end of the 1946-47 season, the Canaries had to seek re-election and a year later, Spiers returned to Ninian Park following the departure of Billy McCandless.

He led City into the First Division in 1951-52 but in 1954 he accepted an offer to manage Crystal Palace, later taking charge at Exeter City and scouting for Leicester City.

SPONSORS

The club's official sponsors are Sports Café. Previous sponsors include Gilesports, Buckley's Brewery, South Wales Echo and Havelet.

The first sponsored game at Ninian Park was the Second Division match against Bolton Wanderers on 9 October 1976 which City won 3-2. The game was sponsored by Barr Soft Drinks Ltd.

STANSFIELD, FRED

Due to the Second World War, Fred Stansfield did not turn professional with the Bluebirds until he was 24. He made his debut at centre-half in a 2-1 defeat at Norwich City on the opening day of the 1946-47 season and missed just one game in that campaign as City won the Third Division (South) championship. His form the following season was so impressive that he was capped by Wales at full international level for the match against Scotland. He scored his only goal for the club in a 4-3 home defeat by Chesterfield on 6 November 1948 but ten matches later he broke his leg in a 3-0 defeat at home to Barnsley.

Stansfield who had played in 111 first team games, was unable to break

Cardiff City 1998-99 squad

back into the side as Cyril Spiers, the City manager, had bought Stan Montgomery from Southend United.

In September 1949 he joined Newport County and went on to play in 21 League games for the Somerton Park club, later becoming their manager. He held this post for a number of seasons, his best being 1951-52 when County finished sixth in the Third Division (South).

STEVENS, GARY

Gary Stevens played his early football for Evesham before being signed by Cardiff City in the summer of 1978. He made his debut for the club in a 7-1 defeat at Luton Town on 16 September 1978 but then went on to score 13 goals in 32 League games including one on his home debut a week later when Blackburn Rovers were beaten 2-0.

In 1978-79 he was the club's joint top scorer with 11 goals which included him finding the net in five successive games at the start of the season. Though the club were relegated from the Second Division in 1981-82, Stevens top scored with 13 League goals including a hat-trick in a 5-4 win over Cambridge United.

At the end of that season, Stevens, who had scored 51 goals in 160 games for the Ninian Park club, left to join Shrewsbury Town for a fee of

£20,000. It was a bargain, for the Birmingham-born player who could play at both centre-half and centre-forward, scored 29 goals in 150 League games for the Gay Meadow club. He then joined Brentford before moving to Hereford United to end his League career.

A former worker in a Herefordshire chicken factory, he had scored 93 goals in 426 League games for his four clubs.

STEWART, FRED

Fred Stewart was involved in the administrative side of Stockport County for a number of years before becoming the club's first manager following their successful application to join the Football League in 1900. Despite Stewart's shrewd dealings in the transfer market, County struggled to stay in the League and finally lost their place in 1904 when they were not re-elected and went to play in the Lancashire Combination. A year later they returned to the League with Stewart not only guiding them to tenth place, their best-ever League position but also helping the club make a profit of £500 on the season.

In May 1911, Fred Stewart was engaged by Cardiff City to become their first secretary-manager. He brought with him a wealth of experience and knowledge to Ninian Park and in 1913 the club won the Second Division of the Southern League. He appointed George Latham as his trainer but his greatest capture without doubt was Billy Hardy from his former club. City did well in the top division of the Southern League, finishing third in 1914-15 and fourth in 1919-20.

Following the club's entry to the Football League in 1920, Stewart signed players from all over the country and had a number of internationals playing for him throughout the 1920s.

The club gained promotion to the First Division in their first season in the Football League. City finished fourth in the top flight in 1922-23 and were unlucky not to clinch the League title the following season. They were beaten finalists in the 1925 FA Cup Final and in 1927 they won the Cup to become the first and only club to take the trophy out of England. This was the height of Stewart's managerial career at Ninian Park, for within four years they found themselves in the Third Division (South).

He decided to retire in May 1933 to concentrate on his business interests and remained living in Cardiff until his death in 1954.

STITFALL, RON

In a playing career which spanned two decades, Ron Stitfall joined his home-town club Cardiff City as a schoolboy during the Second World War and played his first game for the club in wartime competition whilst only 14 years of age.

He appeared in a number of wartime games for the club before serving in the Army for four years. It was 1947 when he returned to Ninian Park and in October of that year, he made his debut at left-back in place of Alf Sherwood who was on international duty in a goalless draw at Brentford. For the next 18 seasons, Stitfall was a virtual ever-present in the Bluebirds side, although in his first few seasons with the club, he played in a variety of positions.

In 1949-50 he had a spell playing centre-forward and scored in each of his first five appearances in that position. Considering he only scored eight goals in the 454 first team games in which he played, it was a remarkable performance.

Surprisingly, he won only two full international caps for Wales, against England in 1952 and Czechoslovakia in 1957. He partnered Alf Sherwood at full-back for nine years and joined Newport County's training staff in 1970.

SUBSTITUTES
The first ever Cardiff City substitute was David Summerhayes who came on for Colin Baker against Bury at Ninian Park on 21 August 1965. The club had to wait until 16 October 1965 for their first goalscoring substitute - George Johnston scoring in the 2-1 home defeat by Portsmouth. The greatest number of substitutes used in a single season by Cardiff under the single substitute rule was 37 in 1985-86, but from 1986-87 two substitutes were allowed, and in 1994-95, 71 were used. For the last few seasons, three substitutes have been allowed, and in 1997-98, the club used 87. The greatest number of substitute appearances for the Bluebirds has been made by Tarki Micallef who came on during 29 League games. It was during 1997-98 that Steve White rewrote the Cardiff records on the matter of substitutes with an extraordinary 17 League appearances in the substitute's shirt.

SULLIVAN, DEREK
One of the most versatile of Cardiff City players, Derek Sullivan made his League debut in a 1-1 home draw against Newcastle United on 10 April 1948 at the age of 17 years 243 days. He played on the left-wing in that game but over the next few seasons he played in all the forward positions before settling into a half-back position in 1952-53. However, he still went

on to play in almost every outfield shirt for the Bluebirds in a career which saw him score 21 goals in 305 games.

His best season in terms of goals scored was the club's promotion winning season of 1959-60 when he scored eight goals in 30 League appearances.

Capped 17 times by Wales, the Newport-born player made his full international debut against Northern Ireland in 1953.

Leaving Ninian Park in September 1961, Sullivan joined Exeter City but after 44 League appearances for the Grecians he returned to South Wales to play for Newport County, where he ended his League career. After a season playing for Hereford United he signed for Welsh League club, Ebbw Vale.

SUNDAY FOOTBALL

Cardiff City played their first Sunday match on 6 December 1981 in a third round Welsh Cup tie at Bridgend. Two goals from Micallef and one apiece from Lewis and Sugrue gave the Bluebirds a 4-1 win in front of a 1,000 crowd.

SUSTAINED SCORING

In 1931-32, Jim McCambridge set a new club record when he scored 26 goals in 37 League games for the Bluebirds. Three times he scored goals in four successive matches and towards the end of the season, scored 12 goals in only seven League games, including hat-tricks against Queen's Park Rangers (Away 3-2) and Clapton Orient (Home 5-0).

McCambridge's record was broken by Stan Richards in 1946-47 as the club won the Third Division (South) championship and still stands. He scored 30 goals in 34 League games including a spell of netting in five successive games. His only hat-trick that season came in a 6-1 thrashing of Norwich City at Ninian Park.

SUTTON, MEL

Mel Sutton was signed from Aston Villa where he was an amateur by Cardiff City manager Jimmy Scoular in December 1967, though he had to wait until the start of the 1968-69 season before making his first team debut. That came in a 1-0 home defeat by Charlton Athletic on 14 August 1968 after which he was a virtual ever-present for the next four seasons. The hard-tackling midfielder went on to play in 178 first team games for the Bluebirds before surprisingly being allowed to leave Ninian Park in the summer of 1972 to join Wrexham for £15,000.

He scored the only goal of the game on his debut for the Robins at

Southend United and soon proved to be one of the game's great bargains. In nine seasons as a player at the Racecourse Ground he appeared in 469 games and in 1977-78 when the club won the Third Division championship and reached the sixth round of the FA Cup Sutton played in every game. During that season, Sutton became player/assistant-manager to Arfon Griffiths and when Griffiths resigned his post in May 1981, he was appointed manager in his place. He was relieved of his duties at the end of the 1981-82 season after Wrexham finished 21st in the Second Division and were relegated.

He joined Arfon Griffiths at Crewe Alexandra but after a short stay at Gresty Road, he left the game.

SWANSEA CITY

The club's arch rivals are Swansea City. The Bluebirds played at the Vetch Field in the Swans' first Southern League match on 7 September 1912 and Jack Burton netted for Cardiff in a 1-1 draw. The return at Ninian Park later in the season was goalless.

The two clubs first met in the Football League on 5 October 1929 at Ninian Park in a game that was also without a goal. The Swans won the return at the Vetch Field 1-0. City's first League victory over Swansea came on 27 December 1930 when a Leslie Jones goal separated the teams. There then followed a 27-year gap before the clubs met in the League again and after a goalless draw at Ninian Park on the opening day of the 1957-58 season, a Colin Hudson goal gave City the points in the return. In 1962-63, City beat Swansea 5-2 and in 1964-65 won 5-0 with Ivor Allchurch scoring a hat-trick and John Charles the other two goals. City in fact, won eight and drew six of the first 15 meetings at Ninian Park, their only home defeat until 1989-90 coming on 7 March 1959.

The clubs have met twice in the FA Cup with the Swans winning on both occasions and once in the League Cup in 1985-86 when the Vetch Field club won 4-3 on aggregate. The two sides also met in the Sherpa Van Trophy of 1988-89 when goals from Curtis and Gilligan gave City a 2-0 win.

Cardiff have also played Swansea in the Welsh Cup on numerous occasions, many of the meetings producing memorable games. On 25 February 1960, City fielded their reserve team in a sixth round tie at the Vetch Field because the Welsh FA refused to change the date of the match even though the Bluebirds had an important League match at Leyton Orient two days later. Swansea fielded their full strength line-up but the Second Division side went behind to a Steve Mokone goal.

As the game wore on, tempers became frayed and the tackles more vigorous, but to the Swans dismay Harry Knowles put City 2-0 up with just 15 minutes to play. The Swans pulled a goal back before Colin Hudson was sent off for dangerous play. A few minutes later, City were reduced to nine men when Mokone and Swansea's Harry Griffiths were dismissed after throwing mud at each other ! The Bluebirds hung on to win 2-1 but they were fined £350 by the Welsh FA and ordered to play their strongest side in the Welsh Cup in future.

In the 1965-66 Welsh Cup competition the teams had drawn 2-2 at the Vetch Field and returned to Ninian Park for the fifth round replay. With just eight minutes of the second half played, Cardiff were 3-0 up and seemingly coasting into the next round. However, in the 64th minute, the game turned on its head when Don Murray received his marching orders. Within a minute, the Swans had pulled a goal back through Todd, who later netted a second and after Herbie Williams equalised, the game went into extra-time. Further goals from McLaughlin and Evans gave the Swans a remarkable 5-3 win.

The two clubs last met on Sunday 8 March 1998 at the Vetch Field when a goal from Jason Fowler gave City a share of the points.

Below are Cardiff's statistics against Swansea:

	P.	W.	D.	L.	F.	A.
Southern League	4	1	2	1	3	3
Football League	40	13	12	15	51	54
FA Cup	2	0	0	2	1	4
League Cup	2	1	0	1	3	4
Sherpa Van Trophy	1	1	0	0	2	0
Welsh Cup	32	17	8	7	59	40
TOTAL	81	33	22	26	119	105

SWINDIN, GEORGE

Goalkeeper George Swindin played for both Rotherham United and Bradford City before joining Arsenal for £4,000 in 1936. In 1937-38 he won the first of three League Championship medals when playing in the last 17 games of the season. In 1946-47 he became the club's first choice 'keeper and in the following League Championship-winning season of 1947-48 he was ever-present, conceding only 32 League goals, which at the time was a new Division One record. He won an FA Cup winners' medal in 1950 when Arsenal beat Liverpool and went on to appear in 299 League and

Cup games for the Gunners.

In February 1954 he joined Peterborough United as player-manager before returning to Highbury as manager in the summer of 1958. Unable to find much success in his four years with the club, he resigned in May 1962 to take charge at Norwich City.

Manager at Carrow Road for only 20 games, he received a much more lucrative offer from Cardiff City and in October 1962 took over the reins at Ninian Park. After John Charles was signed from AS Roma against his wishes, Swindin was dismissed, despite the club winning the Welsh Cup and entering Europe for the first time.

T

TALBOT, LES

Inside-forward Les Talbot began his career with his home-town club Hednesford before being given a chance at Football League level by Blackburn Rovers. Though his opportunities were somewhat limited in his first few years at Ewood Park, he eventually established himself in the side and when he joined Cardiff City in 1936 he had scored 21 goals in 86 League outings for the Lancashire club.

Talbot made his debut for the Ninian Park club in a 1-0 defeat at Walsall on the opening day of the 1936-37 season and over the next three seasons scored some vital goals in what were improved performances by the Bluebirds. He left City at the end of the 1938-39 season, having scored 25 goals in 125 games to join Walsall.

He played in the first three games of the abandoned 1939-40 season before 'guesting' for Bath City during the war. When peacetime football returned in 1946-47 he had one season with the Saddlers before leaving League football.

TALLEST PLAYERS

It is impossible to say for definite who has been the tallest player ever on Cardiff City's books as such records are notoriously unreliable. But almost certain to lay claim to the distinction are goalkeeper John Davies and forwards Rob Turner and Graham Withey who all attained the height of 6ft 3ins.

TAPSCOTT, DEREK

Derek Tapscott joined Arsenal from Barry Town where he was a prolific goalscorer in October 1953. He made his League debut against Liverpool at Highbury in April 1954, scoring twice. During that summer he won the first of his 14 Welsh caps when he played against Austria.

He won a regular place in the Arsenal League side in 1954-55, scoring 13 goals in 37 games. In 1955-56, Tapscott was the Gunners' leading scorer with 21 goals and the following season he scored 25 League goals, the most since Ronnie Rooke netted 33 in 1947-48. Tapscott sustained a number of injuries to his knee and ankle, resulting in him missing the majority of the 1957-58 season. After regaining full fitness he couldn't reclaim his first team place and was sold to Cardiff City for £15,000.

Though he failed to score on his debut in a 4-1 home win over Grimsby Town, he was the club's leading scorer with 20 League goals in 1959-60 as the Bluebirds won promotion to the First Division.

He was the club's top scorer again the following season with 21 goals in 39 League games including his first hat-trick for the club as West Bromwich Albion were beaten 3-1.

Though City were relegated in 1961-62 Tapscott netted his second hat-trick for the club in a 3-2 home win over Birmingham City. He netted his third League hat-trick the following season in a 4-2 win at Charlton Athletic.

Tapscott continued to score on a regular basis and in seven years at Ninian Park he netted 99 goals in 233 first team games including six in the 16-0 Welsh Cup defeat of Knighton in 1960-61 - still the individual scoring record of any City player in a first team fixture. In July 1965 he joined Newport County before later moving into non-League football.

TELEVISION

Cardiff City first appeared on BBC's 'Match of the Day' on 4 January 1969 in a third round FA Cup tie against Arsenal at Ninian Park. The game which was watched by a crowd of 55,136 was goalless before the Gunners won the replay 2-0 three days later.

City's second appearance on the 'Match of the Day' programme on 8 February 1969 saw them defeat Oxford United 5-0 with goals from Clark (2) Toshack (2) and Bird.

THIRD DIVISION

Cardiff City have had seven spells playing in the Third Division although four of them have been for one season only ! The club's first season in the Third Division was 1931-32 and saw them record their biggest win in the Football League when Thames Association were beaten 9-2. After finishing 19th the following season, City had to apply for re-election in 1933-34 after finishing bottom of the Third Division (South). In the years leading up to the Second World War, City finished no higher than 10th but in 1946-47 they won the championship. The Bluebirds scored 93 goals with Stan Richards setting a new club record with 30 goals including a hat-trick in the 6-1 home win over Norwich City.

The club's second spell in the Third Division lasted just one season as they remained unbeaten in their last nine matches to finish the 1975-76 season as runners-up to Hereford United. City's third spell also lasted just one season as in 1982-83 another late run saw them go up as runners-up to Portsmouth.

The club's fourth spell in the Third Division again lasted just one season, but this time the Bluebirds were relegated to the Fourth Division for the first time in their history. City's fifth spell lasted two seasons after finishing 16th in 1988-89, the club were relegated to the League's basement for a second time the following season. In 1992-93, following reorganisation by the Football League, City won the new Third Division championship with 83 points, three more than fellow Welsh club, Wrexham. Following relegation in 1994-95, the Bluebirds have spent the last three seasons playing in the Third Division, reaching the play-offs in 1996-97 where they lost 4-2 on aggregate to Northampton Town.

THIRLAWAY, BILLY

Born in Durham, right-winger Billy Thirlaway played his early football with Unsworth Colliery before joining South Shields. After some impressive performances, the speedy winger was signed by West Ham United and made his Football League debut for the Hammers in 1921. He then had spells with Southend United and Luton Town before joining Birmingham City who were then a First Division club. Unable to settle at St Andrews, he joined Cardiff City in March 1927 and made his debut in a 2-2 draw at Sunderland. Having played in an earlier round of the FA Cup with Birmingham, he was unable to face Arsenal in the FA Cup Final which of course City won 1-0.

In 1927-28 he showed outstanding form as City finished sixth in the First Division, scoring nine goals in 40 League games. Also that season he was in the City side that beat Corinthians 2-1 to lift the FA Charity Shield.

He went on to score 23 goals in 122 games before leaving Ninian Park to play non-League football for Tunbridge Wells Rovers.

THOMAS, ROD

After playing with Gloucester City, Rod Thomas began his League career with Swindon Town, signing for the Wiltshire club in the summer of 1964. In nine years at the County Ground he made 296 appearances and was a member of the Swindon team which beat Arsenal in the 1969 League Cup

Rod Thomas on international duty with 50 caps to his credit

Final. His performances for the Robins eventually led to him being transferred to Derby County in November 1973 for a fee of £80,000.

Though he had to wait to make his mark at the Baseball Ground, an injury to Ron Webster let Thomas into the Rams' side and in the second half of the club's 1974-75 Championship-winning season, he was at last able to show his quality.

The winner of 50 Welsh caps, he joined Cardiff City for just £10,000 in October 1977 and made his debut the following month in a 2-0 home win over Stoke City. Able to play anywhere in the back four, he was deceptively quick and though injury problems hampered his progress at Ninian Park, he made 96 League appearances in four years before rejoining Gloucester City in 1981. He later had a short spell with Newport County before leaving Somerton Park to play non-League football.

TIDDY, MIKE

Mike Tiddy began his career with Torquay United in November 1946 and spent four years at Plainmoor before joining Cardiff City in November 1950. A hard-working unselfish winger, Tiddy was a good crosser of the ball and went straight into City's Second Division team, making his debut in a goalless draw at Barnsley. Over the next five seasons, Tiddy was a regular member of the Bluebirds' first team and played in 163 games, scoring 26 goals before leaving Ninian Park along with Gordon Nutt in September 1955 to sign for Arsenal for a joint fee of £30,000.

He was plunged straight into first team action at Highbury, initially on his natural right side but later more often on the left. Despite enjoying a run of 21 matches in 1955-56 he failed to establish himself and in the end, after undergoing a cartilage operation, was reduced to vying for the left-wing position with Nutt and Joe Haverty.

In October 1958 he left the Gunners to join Brighton and Hove Albion, for whom he performed most creditably, scoring 11 goals in 134 games, before becoming a village postmaster in his native Cornwall.

TONG, DAVID

Midfielder David Tong began his career with his home-town team, Blackpool and made his League debut in the opening match of the 1974-75 season at Norwich City. He went on to score seven goals in 89 games for the Bloomfield Road club before joining Shrewsbury Town in September 1978.

In four years at Gay Meadow, Tong was a virtual ever-present, appearing in 199 first team games and finding the net on 11 occasions.

He joined City on a free transfer in the summer of 1982 and played his first game in Cardiff colours in a 2-1 home defeat by Wrexham on the opening day of the 1982-83 campaign. He went on to appear in 43 games as the Bluebirds won promotion to the Second Division and then in 1983-84 was one of only two ever-presents. He had played in 141 first team games for the club when he was allowed to leave Ninian Park in September 1985. He had short spells with Bristol City, Gillingham and Cambridge United before entering non-League football with Merthyr Tydfil.

TOSHACK, JOHN

One of the greatest names in Welsh soccer history, John Toshack, came off the bench on 13 November 1965 to score the final goal in a 3-1 home win over Leyton Orient - he was just 16 years 236 days old.

A week later he netted twice in a 4-3 win at Middlesbrough and ended the season with six goals in seven games. Over the next few seasons he continued to find the net and on 16 January 1968 he netted his first hat-trick for the club in an 8-0 Welsh Cup win over Ebbw Vale. After teaming up with Brian Clark he netted 31 goals in 1968-69 including scoring in both legs of the Welsh Cup Final in a 5-1 aggregate win over Swansea Town and was the Second Division's leading scorer. In 1969-70 he scored his first League hat-trick for the Bluebirds in a 4-2 home win over Queen's Park Rangers and followed it with another early the next season as Hull City were beaten 5-1.

When he left Ninian Park to sign for Liverpool for £110,000 in November 1970, he had scored 100 goals in 203 games and was already a Welsh international, having been capped against Scotland in 1969.

He quickly endeared himself to the Liverpool fans by helping the Reds come from two goals behind to beat Everton 3-2. He went on to play an important role in winning six major trophies, yet for most of his Anfield career in which he scored 95 goals in 245 games, he was dogged by a nagging thigh injury. His most prolific term was 1975-76 when he found the net 23 times including three hat-tricks on his way to a League title and UEFA Cup double.

After being allowed to leave Anfield in 1977, he joined Swansea City as player-manager and took the Vetch Field club from the Fourth Division to the top of the First Division. Sadly, the club began to slide down the League and Toshack lost his job, despite being awarded the MBE for his achievements in the game. He later managed Sporting Lisbon, Real Sociedad and Real Madrid, whom he took to a Spanish League Championship.

John Toshack takes a penalty against Coventry City
Cardiff City 1 Coventry City 1 - 22nd April 1967 (Att: 19,592)

TOURS

The club embarked on their first overseas tour at the end of the 1923-24 season, taking in Czechoslovakia, Austria and Germany. In Czechoslovakia they played Sparta Prague twice, losing their first meeting 3-2 but then winning by the same scoreline some 24 hours later.

When City visited Denmark in the summer of 1928 it was agreed that substitutes could be used during the tour matches - the first time that such a course of action had been taken. The Bluebirds won all three tour games - Aarhus 2-0, Aalborg 4-0 and Odense 4-1.

One tour that didn't take place was the club's proposed visit to East Germany in 1960. Due to the U2 plane incident, the communists decided to close the border and City had to return home !

TRANSFERS

The club's record transfer fee paid is £180,000 to San Jose Earthquakes for Godfrey Ingram in September 1982. The record transfer fee received by the club is £300,000 from Sheffield United for the services of Nathan Blake in February 1994.

TURNER, BERT

After playing non-League football with Denaby United, Sheffield-born left-winger Bert Turner began his Football League career with Hull City. Never an automatic choice for the Tigers, he moved on to Walsall and in two years for the Midlands club, he scored 21 goals in 56 League games. It was this kind of form that led to Doncaster Rovers signing him in the summer of 1933.

In his first season for the Belle Vue club he scored 26 goals including five against New Brighton as the Yorkshire club went on to win the Third Division (North) championship. He had scored 52 goals in 119 games when he joined Cardiff City in 1937.

His first game for the Bluebirds was in a 1-1 draw at Clapton Orient on the opening day of the 1937-38 season, a campaign in which he scored 19 goals in 40 League games, many of them powerful left-foot drives. Though he scored against Exeter City in the opening game of the following season, he only made one more appearance before leaving to join Bristol Rovers.

John Toshack

U

UNDEFEATED

Cardiff City have remained undefeated at home throughout just one Football League season and that was in 1946-47 when they won the Third Division (South) championship. The club's best and longest undefeated sequence in the Football League at Ninian Park is of 27 matches between 10 April 1939 and 6 September 1947. City's longest run of undefeated Football League matches home and away is 21 between 21 September 1946 and 8 March 1947.

UNIQUE TREBLES

Cardiff City achieved a unique treble on three consecutive Saturdays in 1924. On each occasion they beat Arsenal, winning 2-1 at Highbury in a First Division match on 19 January, 4-0 at Ninian Park the following week in another First Division game and 1-0 on 2 February in the second round of the FA Cup, also played at Ninian Park.

City also achieved a unique treble in 1927 when they made history by winning the Welsh Cup, FA Cup and Charity Shield in the same year.

The Bluebirds drew Leeds United in the third round of the FA Cup in three successive years 1956, 1957, 1958, winning 2-1 in each occasion at Elland Road.

UNUSUAL GOALS

The opening game of the 1963-64 season against Norwich City at Ninian

Park provided one of the most unusual goals in the Football League. With the score at 1-1, City's John Charles, who was making his debut for the Bluebirds, took an indirect free-kick from about 75 yards. The ball was hit deep into the Norwich penalty area, where it bounced and spun into the net off the shoulder of the Canaries' debutant 'keeper Kevin Keelan. Though it was technically an 'own goal' John Charles was credited with having scored. Keelan who went on to make a record number of appearances for the Carrow Road club must have been mortified, for if he hadn't touched the ball, the outcome would have been a goal-kick for the visitors. For the record, Ivor Allchurch netted a third goal to give City a 3-1 win over their East Anglian opponents.

Another unusual goal occurred on 14 December 1968 when City entertained League leaders Millwall at Ninian Park. A John Toshack goal separated the teams, but in the last minute, the Bluebirds scored a second goal when Millwall 'keeper Bryan King's goal-kick was headed straight back over his head and into an empty net by Brian Clark !

City in action against Wrexham

UTILITY PLAYERS

A utility player is one of those gifted footballers who can play in several or even many, different positions. Ron Stitfall, who played his first game for the club during the wartime season of 1942-43 and went on to appear in 403 League games. Derek Sullivan also played in a variety of roles, wearing every shirt except the goalkeeper's and centre-forward.

After the mid-1960s, players were encouraged to become more adaptable and to see their roles as less stereotyped. At the same time however, much less attention came to be paid to the implication of wearing a certain numbered shirt and accordingly, some of the more versatile players came to wear almost all the different numbered shirts at some stage or another, although this did not necessarily indicate a vast variety of positions. In the modern game, Brian Attley and Mike Ford have been talented enough to wear a variety of outfield shirts.

V

VAUGHAN, NIGEL

Nigel Vaughan began his Football League career with Newport County and went on to score 32 goals in 224 League appearances for the Somerton Park club. At Newport he won the first of 10 Welsh caps when he played against Yugoslavia.

He arrived at Ninian Park in September 1983 as part of an unusual five-man exchange deal between the two clubs but suffered an unhappy debut as the Bluebirds lost at home to Barnsley 3-0. He then played in all the remaining 36 games of the season as the club finished 15th in the Second Division. In 1984-85, he was City's top scorer with 16 League goals but despite his efforts, the club were relegated to the Third Division. He was the club's top scorer again the following season but the Bluebirds were relegated for a second successive season and dropped into the League's basement. In 1986-87 he became dissatisfied with Fourth Division football and played on a weekly contract until, after scoring 54 goals in 178 games, he left to join Wolverhampton Wanderers for a fee of £12,000.

He made his debut for the Molineux club at Ninian Park when he came on as a substitute and scored in a 3-2 win for the Bluebirds. He went on to score 10 goals in 93 League outings for Wolves before ending his career with Hereford United.

VEARNCOMBE, GRAHAM

Cardiff-born goalkeeper Graham Vearncombe played his first game for the club on the final day of the 1952-53 season in a 2-0 defeat at Aston Villa. However, over the next two seasons, he only appeared in 17 League games as he understudied Ron Howells, eventually becoming the club's first choice 'keeper midway through the 1955-56 campaign. That season also saw him win a Welsh Cup winners' medal as Swansea Town were beaten 3-2 in the final. In 1957-58 he shared the goalkeeping duties with Ken Jones but the following season, he only played in the final game of the campaign as the club's cricketing 'keeper Ron Nicholls took over between the posts. However, he was the club's 'keeper in all bar one of the games in their run to lifting the Welsh Cup and won his second medal in that competition as Lovell's Athletic were beaten 2-0.

He became the club's number one 'keeper again in 1959-60 and went on to appear in 238 first team games, making his last appearance in the 2-0 Welsh Cup Final replay win over Bangor City in May 1964 to win his third medal.

Vearncombe who won two caps at full international level for Wales, left the Bluebirds in the close season to play part-time football for Merthyr Tydfil.

VICTORIES IN A SEASON - HIGHEST
In 1946-47, Cardiff won 30 of their 42 League fixtures to win the Third Division (South) Championship, the highest in the club's history.

VICTORIES IN A SEASON - LOWEST
Cardiff's poorest performances were in season's 1928-29 and 1930-31 when they only won eight matches out of their 42 League games and were relegated from the First and Second Division respectively.

WAKE, HARRY

Signed from Newcastle United, he made his first team debut in a 1-1 draw at Tottenham Hotspur in February 1924 and went on to play in 12 of the last 14 games of a season that saw City finish runners-up in the First Division. In 1924-25 he faced competition from Joe Nicholson but Wake's form was such that he played in all of the club's eight FA Cup matches as they reached the Final where they lost 1-0 to Sheffield United. One of the starts in the club's run to the final, he made the mistake that resulted in the only goal of the game. He intercepted a pass from United winger Billy Gillespie whilst facing towards his own goal but as he turned with the ball Fred Tunstall took the ball off his toes and ran on to shoot past Tom Farquharson.

In the FA Cup competition of 1926-27 he scored one of the goals in the 3-0 semi-final win over Reading but had to miss the final when he damaged his kidneys in a 3-2 win over Sheffield Wednesday, a match in which he scored one of the goals.

Thankfully, despite a London newspaper reporting his death, he went on to play for Cardiff City until 1931, when after 181 appearances, he joined Mansfield Town where he ended his career.

WALSH, BRIAN

Winger Brian Walsh was playing for Chase of Chertsey when he joined Arsenal as an amateur in March 1949, turning professional five months later. He had appeared in youth team friendly matches for the club when he was called up for National Service in 1950. On his return to Highbury in 1952 he won a regular place in the club's Football Combination side before making his first team debut against Cardiff City in September 1953. However, over the next two seasons he only made 17 League appearances and in September 1955 he joined the Bluebirds in the deal that took Gordon Nutt and Mike Tiddy to Highbury.

He made his debut in a 2-1 win at Preston North End and went on to thrill the Ninian Park faithful with his brilliant ball play for six seasons, scoring 41 goals in 240 games. He won two Welsh Cup winners' medals in 1956 and 1959, scoring two goals in the 3-2 win over Swansea Town in 1956.

In November 1961 he left Ninian Park to play for Newport County for a fee of £2,000. He scored four goals in 27 outings for the Somerton Park club before hanging up his boots.

WARBOYS, ALAN

A big bustling centre-forward, Alan Warboys began his Football League career in his native Yorkshire with Doncaster Rovers and after scoring 12 goals in 39 League appearances was promptly signed by Sheffield Wednesday. The Owls were then a First Division club but when they lost their top flight status in 1970, Warboys, who had scored 13 goals in 71 games was allowed to leave Hillsborough.

Cardiff City manager Jimmy Scoular paid £42,000 to take Warboys to Ninian Park and he made his debut in a 1-1 draw at home to Swindon Town in December 1970. His next game in Cardiff colours was at home against his former club, Sheffield Wednesday, and he scored two goals in a 4-0 win for the Bluebirds.

He ended that 1970-71 season in which City finished third in Division Two with 13 goals in 17 League games, including all four in the 4-0 defeat of Carlisle United. He continued to find the net in 1971-72 and scored a hat-trick in the 5-2 home win over Preston North End. Early the following season after scoring 28 goals in 73 games, he returned to Yorkshire to play for Sheffield United in an exchange deal that saw Dave Powell and Gil Reece join the Bluebirds.

He was soon on the move again, this time to Bristol Rovers where he had his most successful period, scoring 53 goals in 148 appearances as well as helping the Eastville club to promotion from the Third Division in 1973-74. He then had spells with Fulham and Hull City before ending his career with his first club, Doncaster Rovers.

The much-travelled striker scored 137 goals in 482 League games for his seven clubs.

WARTIME FOOTBALL

Despite the outbreak of war in 1914, the major football leagues embarked upon their planned programme of matches for the ensuing season and these were completed on schedule at the end of April the following year. The season saw City finish third in the First Division of the Southern League.

After playing a number of friendly matches, City joined the South West Combination but these games were not a success due to the railways being used for the War effort and at the end of the 1915-16 season, the club withdrew from competitive matches.

Over the next three seasons, the club concentrated on playing friendlies, although in 1917-18, only three were played and none of them were won !

In contrast to the events of 1914, once war was declared on 3 September 1939, the Football League programme of 1939-40 was immediately suspended and the government forbade any major sporting event, so that for a while there was no football of any description.

In 1939-40 after playing a number of friendly matches, City joined the newly formed South West League and finished the season in seventh place. The following season, City played in the Football League (South) and finished fifth on goal average.

The best result of the season was an 8-0 win over Swansea Town with James and Moore both scoring hat-tricks.

In fact, Billy James scored seven goals when City beat an Army XI 18-1 in a friendly match. In 1941-42, a number of international players 'guested' for City and they ended the season in third place. Both Parker and Weir scored hat-tricks in an 8-2 home win over Bristol City. In 1942-43, City moved into the War League (West) and though they finished third, they were beaten 8-4 at home by Lovell's Athletic who had a very strong side during the war years.

The following season City finished runners-up, before winning the League in 1944-45, losing just one match at Ninian Park and that being 1-0 to Lovell's Athletic on the final day of the season. In 1945-46 the Football League decided to keep the regional leagues and City played in the Third Division (South) - South Division before the Football League returned for the 1946-47 season.

WATKINS, JOHNNY

An England Youth international, he began his League career with Bristol City, making his first team debut for the Ashton Gate club in 1955. Over the next four seasons, the flying left-winger scored 17 goals in 95 League games before surprisingly being allowed to sign for Cardiff City for a fee of £2,500.

He made his debut for the Bluebirds on the opening day of the 1959-60 season, scoring once as City beat Liverpool 3-2 in front of a 32,000 Ninian Park crowd. That campaign saw Cardiff win promotion to the First Division as runners-up to Aston Villa and Watkins was the club's only ever-present, scoring 15 goals.

After playing in 23 First Division games in 1960-61, he left Ninian Park to join Bristol Rovers in a deal which saw Dai Ward sign for the Bluebirds. He seemed to lose his form at Eastville and after making just 23 League appearances, drifted into non-League football first with Chippenham Town and then Welton Rovers.

WATTS-JONES, BEN

Ben Watts-Jones spent 21 years at Swansea Town first as a director and then as Chairman. After helping the Swans in to the Southern League, he was instrumental in helping them gain entry to the Football League in 1920. Watts-Jones also served on the selection committee of the Welsh FA but in 1934 with Cardiff City at its lowest ebb after years of success, he was appointed as secretary-manager in place of Bartley Wilson.

He released all but five of the club's existing playing staff and brought in 17 new players.

In that 1934-35 season, Watts-Jones had to battle against low attendances and had little money to spend as the club finished 19th in the Third Division (South). The following season was no different, the Bluebirds dropping one place to 20th and being knocked out of the FA Cup by non-League Dartford at Ninian Park. Though he did bring in some better players before the start of the 1936-37 season, City still struggled. At the end of that campaign, Billy Jennings who Watts-Jones had brought in as coach, replaced him as manager and he reverted to his place on the club's board of directors.

WEATHER CONDITIONS

Whilst the club has played in snow, ice and thick mud, when they entertained Fulham on 31 January 1925, the game had to be suspended for over ten minutes as the players battled in what were described at the time as monsoon-like conditions. After both teams had agreed to come back out, a goal from Len Davies was enough to give the Bluebirds victory.

WELSH CUP

The Welsh Cup is the third oldest cup competition in the world and was instituted in 1877 with the first final being played at Acton Park, Wrexham on 30 March 1878 when Wrexham beat Druids 1-0.

The Bluebirds first won the trophy in 1912 in only their second year in the competition when they beat Pontypridd after a replay. When Cardiff beat Oswestry 10-0 on 14 March 1923, Len Davies, Jimmy Gill and George Reid each scored a hat-trick. When City won the Welsh Cup for a fifth time in 1927 beating Rhyl 2-0, they completed a unique 'double' in winning

Cardiff City - Welsh Cup Winners 1988-89

Back Row (left to right): Alan Curtis, Jimmy Gilligan, Steve Tupling, John Roberts, Nigel Stevenson, George Wood, Paul Wheeler, Ian Walsh, Phil Bater.
Front Row (left to right): Ian Rodgerson, Brian McDermott, Paul Wimbleton, Nicky Platnauer, Terry Boyle (Captain), Kevin Bartlett, Steve Lynex, Jason Gummer, Mark Kelly.

both the English and Welsh Cups in the same season. When City won the Cup in 1956, beating Swansea Town 3-2 in the final at Ninian Park, a record crowd of 37,000 watched the game. On 28 January 1961, the Bluebirds recorded their biggest win in the Welsh Cup when they beat Knighton Town of the Mid-Wales League at Ninian Park, 16-0 with Derek Tapscott establishing a new club individual scoring record with six goals. In 1965 when the Welsh FA were still working on the points system rather than goals aggregate, City beat Wrexham 5-1 at Ninian Park but lost 1-0 at the Racecourse Ground. The third and deciding match was played at Shrewsbury's Gay Meadow ground with City running out winners 3-0. A year later City were involved in a fifth round match against Swansea which went to a replay. The Bluebirds were 3-0 up but in a bad tempered match they were reduced to ten men when Murray was sent off and contrived to lose the game 5-3 after extra-time !

Cardiff City have appeared in 31 Welsh Cup Finals, winning 21.

Below are the years when the Bluebirds have won the trophy:

1912	Pontypridd	3-0	after a replay
1920	Wrexham	2-1	
1922	Ton Pentre	2-0	
1923	Aberdare Athletic	3-2	
1927	Rhyl	2-0	
1928	Bangor City	2-0	
1930	Rhyl	4-2	after a replay
1956	Swansea Town	3-2	
1959	Lovell's Athletic	2-0	
1964	Bangor City	2-0	after a replay
1965	Wrexham	3-0	after a replay
1967	Wrexham	4-3	on aggregate
1968	Hereford United	6-1	on aggregate
1969	Swansea Town	5-1	on aggregate
1970	Chester	5-0	on aggregate
1971	Wrexham	4-1	on aggregate
1973	Bangor City	5-1	on aggregate
1974	Stourbridge	2-0	on aggregate
1976	Hereford United	6-5	on aggregate
1988	Wrexham	2-0	
1992	Hednesford Town	1-0	

WILLIAMS, GARETH

Gareth Williams was born in Wembley but his family returned to Hengoed where he developed in local schools football along with another player who was to make the grade, Graham Moore. Williams was signed by Cardiff City in the summer of 1961 and gained a regular spot in the Bluebirds' midfield during the 1962-63 season. By 1964 he was club captain and over the next three seasons was a virtual ever-present. He had played in 161 League games and scored 14 goals when in October 1967 he joined Bolton Wanderers for a fee of £45,000.

Despite becoming club captain at Burnden Park he suffered a loss of form which was not helped by a poor disciplinary record. During November 1969 he was suspended by the club for refusing to train whilst claiming that he was being made the scapegoat for Bolton's poor results. He never recaptured the form of his Ninian Park days and in October 1971 he joined Bury for £5,000. He made 42 League appearances for the Shakers before retiring to join the prison service. Later he managed a Fylde coast hotel before moving to live in Gran Canaria where he runs a bar.

WILLIAMS, GLYNN

Hard-tackling defender Glynn Williams began his career with his hometown club Caerau and in 1946 helped them win the Welsh Amateur Cup. Even though he had only played in a handful of games, his form had been impressive and Cardiff had no hesitation in signing him.

He made his debut for the Bluebirds in a 1-0 win at Aldershot in January 1947 during the club's Third Division (South) championship winning season. In the seven games he played in that campaign, the opposition failed to score in five of them. His ability to play in either full-back position or at wing-half led to him missing very few games over the next six seasons. In 1950-51 as City just failed in their bid for promotion to the First Division, his form was such that he was capped at full international level by Wales against Switzerland. It was his only cap.

In 1951-52 he played his part in helping the Bluebirds reach the top flight but at the end of the following season he was released after appearing in 160 first team games. Though he failed to score at League level he did get on the scoresheet in an FA Cup third round tie against West Bromwich Albion in January 1950.

WILLIAMS, ROLEY

Swansea-born forward Roley Williams was signed from Welsh League side

Milford United before his home-town club could offer him terms. Able to play at both outside and inside-right, he made his first team debut in a 1-1 draw at Sheffield Wednesday in April 1949. In 1949-50 he got more of an extended run in the side and went on to give the club seven years good service in which he scored 19 goals in 143 first team appearances. In 1951-52 he provided many of the crosses for Wilf Grant to top score with 26 goals as the Bluebirds won promotion to the First Division, though he did score two in the opening three games of the campaign himself.

Williams suffered with a series of niggling injuries throughout his career and therefore never played a full season. He left Ninian Park in 1956 to join Northampton Town but soon left the County Ground to play non-league football for Bath City. He later joined Lovell's Athletic and played against the Bluebirds in the Welsh Cup Final of 1959 which City won 2-0 with goals from Bonson and Hudson.

WILSON, BARTLEY

The founder of Cardiff City, Bartley Wilson was appointed their secretary in 1910. Wilson who had to get about on crutches had a great knowledge of football and was a sound judge of players and tactics. He had seen the Cardiff club grow from its amateur days as Riverside Cricket Club to a First Division club.

When Fred Stewart retired in May 1933, Wilson stepped in to replace him after 33 years as secretary, but it proved to be a disastrous period for the Ninian Park club as they stayed firmly rooted to the foot of the Third Division (South).

With a playing record of having won just seven and drawn three of their 29 matches, Wilson was relieved of his duties and replaced by Ben Watts-Jones. Wilson then remained at Ninian Park in a backroom capacity.

WILSON, BOB

Goalkeeper Bob Wilson began his career with Aston Villa and made nine League appearances for the Midlands club before becoming Jimmy Scoular's first signing in August 1964. The Birmingham-born 'keeper who cost City £2,000 made his debut in the opening game of the 1964-65 season and kept a clean sheet in a goalless draw at home to Ipswich Town. He missed just two games during that campaign, turning in a number of outstanding performances.

He won a Welsh Cup winners' medal and played in the European Cup Winners' Cup quarter-final tie against Real Zaragoza. The following season he played his part in helping City reach the semi-finals of the Football

League Cup but lost his place after conceding five goals at West Ham in the first leg. The Hammers then proceeded to hit five in the second leg past Wilson's stand-in. He won another Welsh Cup winners' medal in 1966-67 and the following season played in all of the club's nine European Cup Winners' Cup matches.

His performances in this competition helped the Bluebirds reach the semi-final but after some outstanding saves in the first leg in Hamburg, he made a costly error at Ninian Park which allowed the Germans to win 3-2 on the night and 4-3 on aggregate.

Wilson who appeared in 150 first team games for the club, left Ninian Park in January 1970 to join Exeter City where he made 204 League appearances before ending his career.

WOOD, GEORGE
Goalkeeper George Wood joined Blackpool during the 1971-72 season from East Stirling and went on to appear in 129 League and Cup games for the Bloomfield Road club before joining Everton for £150,000 in August 1977.

An ever-present in his first two seasons with the Goodison club, he appeared in 114 consecutive League and Cup games after making his debut in a 3-1 home defeat by Nottingham Forest. He kept 19 clean sheets

George Wood doing what he did best

in 1977-78 and 15 in 1978-79, this form helping him win two Scottish caps whilst with the club. However, midway through the 1979-80 season, he lost his place to Martin Hodge and at the end of the campaign he was allowed to join Arsenal for £150,000.

In three seasons at Highbury he made 70 League and Cup appearances before leaving to play for Crystal Palace. He spent five seasons at Selhurst Park before joining Cardiff City in January 1988.

He made his debut for the Bluebirds in a 4-0 home win over Cambridge United and went on to keep nine clean sheets in 13 appearances in helping the club win promotion from the Fourth Division.

That season he also won a Welsh Cup winners' medal as City beat Wrexham 2-0 in the final. In 1988-89 he missed just one League game as the Bluebirds finished 16th in the Third Division and kept 18 clean sheets including four games in succession. Wood had played in 92 first team games for City when he was granted a free transfer and signed for Hereford United in August 1990.

He later had a loan spell at Blackpool and played for Merthyr Tydfil and Inter Cardiff where he was manager.

WOODRUFF, BOBBY

A member of Swindon Town's successful young side which gained promotion to the Second Division in 1962-63, he made 180 League appearances for the County Ground club before being transferred to First Division Wolverhampton Wanderers for £40,000 in March 1964. Woodruff became known for his long throw 'specials' and after scoring 18 goals in 59 matches for the Molineux club, he was signed by Crystal Palace in the summer of 1966 for £35,000.

He helped Palace to promotion to the First Division in 1968-69 but played only a few games in the top flight before joining Cardiff City in November 1969 for £25,000. At Selhurst Park Woodruff scored 48 goals in 125 League games and, on his arrival at Ninian Park he continued in a similar vein.

He made his debut in a 2-1 home win over Preston North End and over the next five seasons, proved himself a most reliable player, scoring 22 goals in 150 League games for the club. During the 1972-73 season he had a spell playing centre-forward and scored six goals in six games, ending the campaign with 10 from 34 League appearances.

He left Ninian Park in the summer of 1974 and teamed up with Brian Harris at Newport County. He made 52 appearances for the Somerton

Bobby Woodruff

Park club before finishing his career in Welsh League soccer.

WORST STARTS

The club's worst-ever start to a season was in 1989-90. It took nine League games to record the first victory of the season, drawing just two and losing six of the opening fixtures. The run ended with a 3-2 success at Huddersfield Town on 7 October 1989.

In 1921-22, the club's first season in the First Division, City lost their first six matches but recovered to end the campaign in fourth place.

'X'

In football 'x' traditionally stands for a draw. The club record for the number of draws in a season is 23 in 1997-98. There were 16 draws in seasons 1950-51, 1973-74 and 1986-87.

XMAS DAY

There was a time when football matches were regularly played on Christmas Day but in recent years the game's authorities have dropped the fixture from their calendar.

The club's first Southern League fixture to be played on Christmas Day was in 1911 when City beat Croydon Common 4-0. Cardiff's first Christmas Day fixture in the Football League was in 1920, their initial season in the competition when two goals from Jimmy Gill helped the Bluebirds beat Coventry 4-2 at Highfield Road.

The club have also suffered a number of heavy defeats in this fixture, notably in 1926 when they lost 5-0 at Newcastle United, and 1933 when they went down 4-1 at Coventry. The Christmas Day fixture of 1951 saw City play at the Vetch Field in the first meeting of the clubs on this date.

The Bluebirds drew 1-1 with Mike Tiddy netting for Cardiff. The last League match at Ninian Park on Christmas Day was 1954 when City beat West Bromwich Albion 3-2 with two goals from Trevor Ford and one from Stan Montgomery.

Y

YORATH, TERRY

An often under-appreciated member of the great Leeds United side of the late 1960s and early 1970s, the rugged blond Welsh international won 59 caps. After scoring 12 goals in 196 first team games he left Elland Road in August 1976 to join Coventry City for £125,000. Three years later, Tottenham Hotspur paid £275,000 for him and in his first season at White Hart Lane performed admirably. A series of injuries in 1980-81 cost him his place but when fully fit he couldn't reclaim his regular place in the side and he moved to Vancouver Whitecaps.

He was assistant to Trevor Cherry at Bradford City but was then appointed Swansea's manager. He took the Vetch Field club to promotion to the Third Division in 1988 but left the club in controversial circumstances to return to Valley Parade. He paid £18,000 out of his own pocket to honour his contract with the Swans.

He did not last long at Bradford and was dismissed after a string of disappointing results. In a bizarre turn of events he returned to Swansea but was later sacked.

After being appointed Wales national manager he took them close to qualification to the 1992 European Championships before taking charge at Cardiff City, following the sacking of Eddie May. Yorath who was also a director as well as Team Manager was a member of a consortium trying to buy the club, resigned in March 1995 as City ended the campaign in one of the Second Division's relegation places.

YOUNGEST PLAYER

The youngest player to appear in a first-class fixture for Cardiff City is John Toshack who scored one of the Bluebirds' goals in a 3-1 home win over Leyton Orient on 13 November 1965 aged 16 years 236 days.

YOUTH CUP

In 1970-71, the club reached the final of the FA Youth Cup where they met Arsenal over two legs. The young Bluebirds lost 2-0 on aggregate with the leg at Ninian Park being watched by a crowd of over 12,000.

Cardiff City 1982-83
Back row (left to right): Jeff Hemmerman, Roger Gibbins, Phil Dwyer, Jim Brown,
Andrew Dibble, Gary Bennett, Bob Hatton, Paul Maddy.
Front row: Paul Giles, Dave Bennett, David Tong, John Lewis, Jimmy Mullen (Captain),
Constantinous 'Tarki' Micallef, Linden Jones, Paul Bodin.

Z

ZENITH

Few fans will argue over which moment has been the finest in the club's history. On 23 April 1927, Cardiff City became the only team to take the FA Cup out of England when they beat Arsenal 1-0 at Wembley, with Hughie Ferguson scoring the all-important goal for the Bluebirds.

FA Cup Final - Cardiff City 1 Arsenal 0 - April 23rd 1927
Jack Butler, Tom Parker, Len Davies, Dan Lewis

A mid-air collision in a City domestic fixture

Index

Bibliography

Let's Talk about Cardiff City, Tom Morgan, Sentinel, 1946

Cardiff City Football Club - The Official History of the Bluebirds, John Crooks, Yore Publications, 1992

Cardiff City Chronology, 1920-1986, John Crooks, Published by the Author, 1986

A Short History of Cardiff City FC, Western Mail, 1952

Wembley 1927 - Cardiff v Arsenal FA Cup Final 1927, Derrick Jennings & Ceri Stennett, 1987

Photographs have been supplied by Lancashire Evening Post; Peter Stafford; the author's personal collection: pages 3, 22, 23, 35, 44, 50, 75, 110, 140, 158, 163, 177, 179; Richard Shepherd: pages 31, 47 53, 80, 96, 115, 130, 142, 144, 161, 182, 183; and Hill's Welsh Press.

New turf for a new season at Ninian Park

Notes